PLANTATION THEORY

PLANTATION THEORY

THE BLACK PROFESSIONAL'S STRUGGLE BETWEEN FREEDOM & SECURITY

JOHN GRAHAM

This publication is designed to provide competent and reliable information regarding the subject matter covered.

Copyright © 2021 by John Graham.

Mynd Matters Publishing
715 Peachtree Street NE
Suites 100 & 200
Atlanta, GA 30308

ISBN: 978-1-953307-59-0 (pbk)
ISBN: 978-1-953307-60-6 (hdcv)
ISBN: 978-1-953307-61-3 (ebook)

CONTENTS

*To my wife Sana, my son, John III,
and my daughter Marian,
Your love and support through my journey have
been nothing short of astounding. May this serve
as a guide to my children as they traverse the
world as Black professionals one day. Also, to my
parents, John Sr. and Robin Hurd-Graham.
You've each served as the foundation and the
blueprint for who I am both personally and
professionally with love and guidance.*

Thank you!

FOREWORD

I was awakened from a deep and much needed sleep when my cell phone rang. It was a colleague clearly in some level of distress. Even though I was barely conscious and don't recall there being a formal greeting of hello or good morning, through the haze, I heard a question, "How do you manage the stress and trauma of all of the tragedies that are being reported on a daily basis?" I responded with something like, "Well, you have to limit how much of the bad news you listen to. We all need to take care of ourselves and not allow the toxic stuff in." He paused for a moment and said, "That would be difficult for me since it is my job to report the news. I guess I'm like a doctor that can't stand the sight of blood. Thank you for listening, you have a good day Dr. Joy." I went right back to sleep but was awakened by several more unanswered calls and text messages.

It isn't unusual for me to receive calls like the ones that morning because my friends, family and colleagues know about my work of healing the traumatic wounds that African Americans still carry from generations of injury both physical and mental. Injuries sustained from slavery, Jim Crow, mass incarceration, serial displacement, as well as, fresh new wounds from contemporary racial terrorism. This time the trigger was the trial for George Floyd, a black man mercilessly killed before a world audience.

I had a deadline to write the foreword to John Graham's *"Plantation Theory: The Black Professional's Struggle Between Freedom & Security."* But first, I had to reach back out and apologize to my early caller for my abrupt response and to let him know I would be available to help him process the heavy burden he was carrying. This is the 'work'—my work—to heal, advocate, promote justice and try to prevent future injury.

Plantation Theory is timely and deeply impactful, with content that is brilliant, significant, and enlightening. John Graham has provided a unique lens into the world of corporate America, where he reveals some of the usual suspects of the white capitalist power structure, characters that are all too familiar to Black people or perhaps anyone in America regardless of hue. I found myself ruminating about the corporate world and how the author describes the difficult terrain that he, and other Black people have had to navigate in order to remain in white spaces of power, how each man or woman, must determine just how Black they can be and remain valuable, relevant, and ultimately, successful and secure.

Few of us working outside the corporate plantation fully understand the sacrifices necessary to remain in white proximity to influence and advancement. Graham gives an up close, inside view of this modern plantation as he masterfully describes the intricacies of how the process of "othering" takes place. How even in the midst of high praise and congratulatory applause, promotion consistently becomes a dream deferred.

We tell ourselves our stellar education and hard-earned professional experience will be enough to be proffered a seat at the table, but it is rarely enough. This book illustrates how the past has shaped the present, how the toil of our enslaved ancestors and the blanket of terrorism that even now still wraps itself around us, has a cost that doesn't go unnoticed by those closest to us.

With laser-like precision, Graham fuses together our collective cultural memory and experience as he captivatingly describes "the contract" so many of us sign. A tacit agreement to don the cloak of cultural invisibility in exchange for the basement keys to the palace. Still, we are afforded some of the necessary tools needed to survive as the "other" behind the thin veil of corporate professionalism and a normalized inauthentic work life. And as for those that choose to go down this road seeking freedom and security, that are still in touch with their full humanity, do not expect profound remedies but rather intelligent tools that invite critical change and accountability while unmasking the hidden pitfalls and dangerous cracks in the road to avoid along the way.

-Dr. Joy A. DeGruy
Author of *Post Traumatic Slave Syndrome*

PREFACE

I understand how inconceivable it is. The thought that your reality is not the only reality. I can understand how you would never know what it feels like not to be seen or acknowledged because the monuments to your existence are everywhere. I attempt to empathize with your obliviousness. But it's hard. It's like sitting in a movie theater with an audience watching a movie for the first time, but you've already seen it hundreds of times before.

In a quiet collaboration room in an office of a multi-billion-dollar company, I was once asked, "Why don't we trust white folks?" The woman who asked was genuine. She couldn't understand why the system put in place to receive our complaints was severely underutilized. She wanted to help but felt helpless because she couldn't do anything if she didn't know about it. I got up, walked over to the whiteboard, and raised the marker to write. I wrote "400" and stepped back. I looked at her and asked if she knew what the number represented. She shook her head, befuddled. I told her it was the number of years since the first documented slaves touched the shores of the Americas. Then, I went back to the whiteboard and wrote "346." I then asked if she knew what it represented. Again, she shook her head, no. I explained to her that institutions were erected over the course of 346 years to legalize, justify, and normalize slavery, rape, mutilation, killing, dehumanization, incarceration, injustice, and disenfranchisement. I approached the whiteboard one last time and scribbled the number "54." I then told her that number represents the number of years it has been legal for the two of us to sit in a room alone without me being at risk of going to jail or, worse, being brutalized or killed.

Fifty-four years since Native Black people in this country have been recognized as citizens with the rights afforded their white counterparts. My parents were born eleven years before they would be legally known as full citizens. I've witnessed teenagers killed in the street by police and left uncovered for their communities to see. I've seen a fully licensed gun owner killed in front of his girlfriend and their child live on social media only for the police officer who committed such a blatant crime to go unpunished. I've gazed in horror as I watched life be squeezed from a man's lungs for eight minutes and forty-six seconds while an officer knelt on his neck and back. I asked a question in response to her question. "What evidence do we have in the last 400 years to support our belief in the system or those who uphold it?" She sank back in her chair slightly and said, "I understand." She then corrected herself by saying she could never understand, but she certainly got my point.

I've been on a journey of discovery within corporate America. I've experienced the benefits of being a lighter-skinned Black man in spaces that have historically offered preferential treatment to those who are more closely complexioned to the power structure. I've had to correct assumptive statements of being mistaken for mixed-race and, in one case, even arguing with an ignorant white girl fresh out of college who couldn't understand why I went to an HBCU because she wouldn't accept that I was Black. I've been invited in by privilege and confided in by influential people, and to this day, I still can't fully understand why or how. My wife tells me I operate with a sense of entitlement. Almost as if I have a right to be what I want to be and do what I want to do, I sometimes have expectations that borderline arrogance. Maybe I was one of them in a former life.

I have sought most of my adult life to understand the mechanisms of power, wealth, and race. I was an African Studies major and a history minor at the first degree-granting Historically Black College in America. I grew up in predominantly white suburbs due to my parents' income, so this was the first time in my life that my appearance didn't define me. The first time I wasn't an "Other" or had to explain why I brush my hair. It was the first time in my life I got to be part of the majority. For five years, I experienced this feeling. Perhaps that's why I have a sense of entitlement. Or maybe it's what privilege feels like, and I had a taste of it. Albeit brief, it was enough exposure to the feeling of heightened authenticity without fear of judgment or stereotype. It was the feeling of only worrying about my performance and not worrying that my successes or failures would represent every Black person around me. Perhaps it was having historical images of people that looked like me drape the hallways or mark the campus in monuments that filled me with a sense of pride and honor I'd never known previously. In hindsight, I miss those days and don't quite appreciate how rare that experience truly is for a Black person. My wife went to a Historically White Institution (HWI) for undergrad, and to this day, she wishes she could have experienced what it was like to have gone to an HBCU. What I take for granted because I'm a third-generation alumnus, she envies even still.

I've been on a journey as a Black man in corporate America. I've had leaders who've never built global brands praise me for my expertise and creativity and, in the very next breath, put up barriers to projects simply because they had an opinion that conflicted with data-backed research. They'd say things like, "I know this is frustrating, and I don't want you to think this is about you," Or "You have to know you are extremely valued by us and the company. You are making such a tremendous impact." But these statements that run like 8mm films on a loop in my head as I stare at the ceiling at 3 AM don't ever seem to make me feel like I can believe them. I often ask myself how much my years of professional expertise and track record of success mean in the shadow of a white person's opinion? Maybe I shouldn't feel that way, but I've seen too much on this journey. I've lived in the digital age, and I have listened to the experiences of countless people in corporate America who look like me. There's a consistent thread that is woven through each of our experiences, from 1619 to 2021. The remnants of our ancestors' plight still live with us in a mitigated form. An evolved form. To focus on the effects on Black people alone would be to recount a story from only one side. The injustices of Black people are well known to us. We revisit them with every new slave film from Hollywood or M.L.K. reference during Black history month. But no one speaks of the realized effects of 400 years of institutionalized slavery on white people. Dr. Joy DeGruy, in her lecture on Post Traumatic Slave Syndrome, says, "It's the secrets that make us sick." Could it be that centuries of systematic dehumanization has left white people incapable of feeling empathy for Black people? To justify some of the horrific stories of slaughter, rape, and humiliation, it would be impossible not to be affected in some way if you deemed these beings as human.

This is not a solutions book. You won't find the latest tips and tricks to increase diversity at your company, or any en vogue trend-of-the-day approaches to move your organization up the DEI maturity scale. I'm writing this with the highest aspiration that my lived experiences and the lived experiences of those who look like me provide perspective and purpose. I want the humanity of being Black in a space that America designed with our inclusion far from mind to shine through. I want the future generations of Black contributors to know they're living a shared experience but with more opportunity than those who preceded them. I want my children to read this and know they are endowed with the inalienable rights to be their most authentic selves without altering, suppressing, or diminishing their Blackness. To the Black professional, let this serve as the fuel you need to finally get off the modern-day plantation. May this provide the perspective required to reject the premise of the American Dream, and instead define a new Black American reality of ownership, excellence, and communal obligation.

It's my sincerest hope that my friends and colleagues who are not Black can read this with a level of academic curiosity that enables them to reflect on their own biases and misgivings about Black employees and co-workers. I want you to allow yourself the space to grow as a human being through the narratives of others who don't share your entitlement and privilege. I implore you to interrupt your knee-jerk fragility responses and forge through the automatic barriers that, at times, may seem like the best form of self-protection for your ego. I realize some of the upcoming text may challenge your identity and self-awareness to its very core. The reward for reaching the end of this book is a heightened sense of self-clarity and proximal awareness that will enable you to be better leaders, employees, co-workers, neighbors, allies, and, most importantly, human beings.

Chapter One

CODE-SWITCHING:
LEAVE YOUR ETHNICITY AT THE DOOR

'll never forget the day my daughter, then seven years old, asked my wife a question that would leave her helplessly stunned. This inquiry caught her so off guard, she had to defer on answering until she spoke to me. I was just coming off a conference call in our home office when I rounded the corner to the kitchen, and my wife says, "Guess what your daughter just asked me. I didn't know how to answer it. What do you think?" I stopped, thought for a second, and said, "Tell her the truth."

By now, you're probably wondering what question could be so consequential that could come from a seven-year-old's innocent mind. What could give two highly-educated adults pause to the point of serious contemplation? The question she posed was innocuous yet bared the full gravity of a planet all at once.

"Mommy, why do you change your voice when you call the doctor's office or call the school?" Our daughter struck a profundity in this neatly packaged posit that would require us to assemble a united front to counter. As we sat at the dinner table, I asked our daughter to repeat the question she asked Mommy. She did. It still had the same punching power as it had earlier when I heard it second hand. I had a magical response that would solve world peace and end systemic racism in one fell swoop in my head. However, what came out was a simple truth I didn't have a chance to curtail after it left my lips.

"Mommy changes her voice when she talks on the phone to make white people feel more comfortable," I explained in the most digestible way possible for a seven-year-old and our nine-year-old son who was half-listening as he ate and watched tv. I suggested that Black people change who they are in front of white people so the latter don't feel threatened.

This harsh truth may be shocking for some of you, but please know this is the reality for Black folks every day. We have to navigate our entire existence in your presence because so much hangs in the balance. In some cases, our very lives depend on our ability to reduce the perception of threat. In the workplace, our potential for getting the interview, getting hired, or getting promoted are mostly the result of our successful execution of threat perception reduction. Code-switching is defined as *the practice of alternating between two or more languages or varieties of language in conversation.* However, for Black people in corporate spaces, we have to alternate more than our vernacular.

The way we dress, how we wear our hair, the tone of voice we use, and even our vocal pitch can negatively impact our career viability. The president of a multinational Fortune 50 company, a soft-spoken Black man, once shared that just being in the room and silent, as a 6'3" Black man, can be imposing or intimidating. The ugly truth is that our existence is a reminder to white people that we are Black, a glaring example of being "Other."

A study conducted in 2012 showed that working adults who feel the need to suppress their group identity at work were more likely to perceive discrimination at work and were less likely to openly express their specific identity. These experiences resulted in lower job satisfaction and higher turnover *(Medera, King, & Hebl, 2012)*. Now imagine for a moment that this was your reality. Imagine having to account for the outward perception you're generating at *all* times of the day while at work or conference calls. The amount of energy that's required to sustain this existence is beyond fathomable for most. The impact on Blacks' health outcomes in corporate jobs correlates to the added stresses and pressures of having to suppress our identity in white spaces.

Social identity threat leads to vigilance for cues in the environment that people will be psychologically, and even physically, safe. The vigilance consumes precious

*cognitive resources that undermine the employee's
ability to fully engage in their work, which has
consequences for their performance (Murphy et al.,
2013). Moreover, the increased vigilance undermines
mental and physical health (e.g., Clark et al., 1999;
Jones et al., 2016).*

If you're having a hard time believing this one entirely, I'll kindly ask you to take a moment and think back to the last time you were in predominantly Black surroundings. Maybe you were invited to a cookout, found yourself in a Black barbershop, or were at a small venue concert. Try to tap into the feelings you had. Was their anxiety or nervousness? Did you feel fear for your safety? Did you find yourself trying to assimilate into the uncomfortable environment by altering your speech patterns or mannerisms to reflect the majority's culture? If you were there with someone you knew, did you hesitate to speak up or engage for fear of saying the wrong thing? If you've never been in a predominantly Black setting, that begs a different question altogether. Still, if you have been and these feelings I'm describing ring true, you'll have some semblance of understanding what the everyday lived experience is like for Blacks in corporate America. I dare say we expend considerable effort not to fall victim to stereotypical "Blackness" closely related to the images of uneducated field hands in whites' eyes. While that may sound harsh, I must call your attention to history for just a moment.

The earliest scenarios for Blacks and whites coalescing in a workspace together in this country are under the auspices of forced labor, better known as chattel slavery. Our primary connectedness hinges upon the very foundation of work and our earliest working relationship would set the scene for the next 450 years. Now, while we weren't paid for the work we performed for nearly 250 years, we still had to ensure that at no time did the overseer or Master feel a perceived threat from our existence. Even more, for us to showcase an increased value by working extra hard to produce higher outputs could increase the likelihood of being sold at high market value and destroying families. It's out of these and many more scenarios where we've had to tone down our Blackness and assimilate more of our white counterparts' mannerisms into our living lexicon to achieve some semblance of success in corporate America.

As I think back to my earliest days of watching both of my parents traverse the corporate world, I can remember seeing how they molded themselves into different people when they stepped out of the house or answered the phone. I also remember how that affected my sense of self and how I eventually navigated the world outside my home. My mother was an entrepreneur who established a successful telemarketing outsource business. She would hire staff to do outbound cold calling or inbound customer service for corporate clients. Based on the fact that these jobs usually paid $8-$12 an hour, you can imagine that the types of people who would work the phones weren't coming from upper-class neighborhoods. Some were high school dropouts, and others were college students looking to make a bit of extra cash to support themselves. I remember many single moms trying to make ends meet for their children at home. No matter who they were, they had this uncanny ability to become whoever they needed to be when the phone rang, and a potential customer picked up on the other end. This stealthy identity shift was mainly because my mother would develop the scripts for the inbound and outbound calls and train the employees on how to "Give good phone," which was a term she came up with to define great teleservice. At the time, I didn't know she was training them to disarm the person on the other end. It was a powerful tactic that played like an assassin sneaking up behind his target and rendering them utterly defenseless without ever giving up his enemy position. This magical maneuver enabled them to go from Maria to Mary and Javon to James in the blink of an instant, heightening their chances of closing a sale or saving a customer from ending services. I sat fascinated by it all as I would hang out in her office after school. A single mother herself, I'd often have to tag along until the night was over. Seeing all of this had a profound effect on me. I remember getting a call from a recruiter for a job I applied for when I was first out of school. We hit it off and found that we had many things in common as she was also a recent graduate, and it was her first job. A week later, I had an in-person interview. The role was for a door-to-door sales position where I'd be going to various offices in a given territory selling office products from a catalog. I arrived at the makeshift office set up in a former retail space that still had the storefront windows where I can assume mannequins used to showcase the sixties' latest fashions. When I walked in, a young woman behind an office desk, who seemed to be making calls and scheduling appointments, almost simultaneously, smiled and greeted me. I was about fifteen minutes early, so I checked in and introduced myself.

"Hi, I'm John Graham, and I'm here for the interview." She had this look as if she were in both disbelief and shock at the same time. I will never forget the tone of her voice as she said, "You're John Graham? I wasn't expecting...you didn't sound like a..." She struggled to recover without making the visible and awkwardly inappropriate racist justification for her disbelief. She advised me to have a seat, and told me the manager would be with me in just a few moments. I could tell by her voice that this was the very person I had a great connection with over the phone, but alas, it was under seemingly false pretense. My ability to code-switch and become a fully entitled white man named John Graham over the phone left me in no man's land when I arrived in person. The tactics I picked up from watching the master code-switching displays of my mother and her trained tele-spies seemed to only work so long as the person on the other end of the phone never actually saw them. This truth was a part of the lesson I had to learn for myself. Lesson learned.

To create the visual of being a white person in one medium and delivering a Black person in another is an affront to the sensibilities akin to false advertising by a consumer brand. This supposed bait and switch can have damaging effects on Black candidates' hiring potential without ever being brought to light by the recruiter or the hiring manager as the real reason for not advancing their candidacy. The irony of it all is that from a very young age, we're told that when we seek employment, we have to know how to "Speak corporate," which in essence means to sound white, or we won't even get past the front door. This duality requirement is not unique to Black folks as other minorities experience some sense of ethnicity suppression. However, there are no parallels to the Black experience as we cannot turn off our ethnicity in person.

THE JEFFERSON OBAMA DINNER & THE DISADVANTAGED

During a conversation with an executive at my company, I asked about development and what the term means in the context of career advancement. He suggested that the word can take on different meanings based on the needs of the individual. One element, he mentioned, was assimilation development. Not so much the assimilation of culture, but more so to understand how things work at a company, its processes, and leadership expectations. However, that triggered a thought for me about actual assimilation.

I shared an example of some feedback he had provided to me once on a call. I was having challenges with my direct manager's communication style, and things were starting to get a bit hostile as a result. I contended that she doesn't communicate her requests expressly and transparently, which leaves me to guess or fill in the blanks of what she's asking. There always seemed to be double-speak or implied, but not readily tangible, language underneath that I struggled to grasp. These failures, on my part to understand, led to a few miscommunications and her feeling as if I were disobeying direct instructions. His coaching for me was that I needed to learn how to "read the tea leaves" and "weak signals" she was giving. It took me a few months to process his statement, but I never forgot how awkward it sounded. It wasn't until I was on a call with a Black friend at work, and we were talking about code-switching and its requirements to achieve success in corporate spaces that clarity came. When I recalled the statement about tea leaves and weak signals, she responded almost instinctively. She said something so profound and familiar, I felt like kicking myself for not remembering this simple fact. She suggested that we in the Black community don't deal in coded language when engaging. We are direct, transparent, and we say what we mean. Not doing so in the hood, she said, is a sign of weakness, and you'll be labeled a punk as a result mainly because you lack the conviction to say what you think and fear what someone will think or say about you. It reminded me of the various African cultures I'd studied in undergrad and how their languages didn't possess these grey area phrases that the western languages do. There's more of an absoluteness to the ancient cultures that still exists today. Something either is or is not—there is no ambiguity.

This truth connected the dots for me on why I was so put off by the statement when I heard it from the executive. It became more apparent as one of the reasons Black folks have such a hard time rising through the ranks. There is a coded language our schooling failed to teach. The more I thought about it, the more I realized that the Black people I'd seen rise to companies' highest levels didn't speak like most

Black folks I know in the lower levels. They reflected whiteness so well that the only recognizable evidence of their culture was purely their appearance. They had mastered the art of double-speak and coded directives. They cracked the code of how to say something without saying anything. They had learned to weaponize misdirection and magical vernacular tactics that wraps daggers in satin, so their real danger remains concealed in velvety outer robes. This realization signaled to me that this is the level of conformity required to run the plantation.

I was having a conversation with my father regarding the unprecedented times we're living in and how since the murder of George Floyd, we have a small window to make significant changes in corporate America. He shared experiences of being a mid-level manager during his time at Ford Motor Company and his challenges while climbing the corporate ladder. We discussed the necessity of White patronage, but I'll cover that in a later chapter.

He shared an experience when he was based in the field and was coming under a new interim manager. At this point in his career, he was thirty-nine, ironically, the same age I am as I write this. On a business trip to headquarters in Detroit, his new manager invited him to his home to discuss his career. They knew each other through various mutual colleagues, but this would be the first time they'd work together. He explained to my father that he wouldn't be in the role for long and he didn't see him being able to help advance his career much. He told my father flat out that he didn't see him getting a promotion during his tenure under him, and the best he could hope for was a lateral move to another assignment. My father responded in a dignified manner befitting the generations of highly-educated Black men and women of his lineage. He said he didn't expect a promotion. He expected he would be considered based on his track record of delivering results and outstanding performance reviews if an opportunity became available. He didn't expect preferential treatment, he only expected fairness. True to form, he didn't get a promotion under this manager's short tenure. It would be another year or so, and a different manager altogether, before getting the promotion to an executive role. This led us to another discussion about the difficulty of being seen, heard, and valued in white spaces, which led me to share a recent revelation.

I told him about a dinner party that my wife and I had recently hosted. It was a Jefferson Dinner, but in our case, it was a Jefferson/Obama dinner. It followed the format of the tradition that Thomas Jefferson was known for, where he would invite the most brilliant minds in politics, academia, and science to a dinner that would be fueled by a single topic of discussion. He essentially leveraged the collective brainpower of his guests to help solve complex problems. Our dinner's theme was, "Who's responsible for solving systemic racism, and how can it be achieved?" We had several sub-topics to drive the discussion that revolved around community, economics, political influence, media control, and education. The guests were co-workers and their spouses. Each ranged in background and perspective. We had a Nigerian couple, whose experiences, even between the two, were markedly different. The husband was born and raised in Nigeria and immigrated to the U.S. to attend University. His wife was a first-generation Nigerian American and spent her first fourteen years in the States before returning to Nigeria for high school and then returning to America for college. Then there was a fraternity brother of mine who would be described by W.E.B. Du Bois as "The talented 10th." His high-minded ideals were shaped by his education and a world view that saw the possibilities in all things with Black ingenuity and excellence.

Du Bois used the term "the talented tenth" to describe the likelihood of one in ten Black men becoming leaders of their race in the world through methods such as continuing their education, writing books, or becoming directly involved in social change. He strongly believed that Blacks needed a classical education to be able to reach their full potential, rather than the industrial education promoted by the

*Atlanta compromise, endorsed by Booker T.
Washington and some white philanthropists. He saw
classical education as the basis for what, in the 20th
century, would be known as public intellectuals.*

Then we had a couple who we have come to know as family friends. They grew up in Inglewood and Oakland, California, respectively. Raised in the "hood," but their work ethic and their brilliance elevated their station, and they were now living in one of the most affluent zip codes in Southern California.

At this point in the conversation, I explained the dynamic of the backgrounds in the room to my father. I suggested that they were a mix of "Black Elite" and "Lower socio-economic" to describe the group's upbringings and social origins. He stopped me and said that those terms didn't sound right, and he suggested that "Advantaged" and "Dis-Advantaged" would be more suitable. I listened as he described friends he grew up with who had many of the same opportunities. Still, at some point, they chose a different path that didn't end up in success based on their parents not being educated and pushing their children towards success. As I listened, I could identify several friends in my circle who fit the same description. Brilliant beyond all measure, but at some point, they veered from a path and made choices that, in some cases, set them back significantly. I quickly saw a common denominator between the friends my father spoke of and those in my circle. I suggested that at a 50,000-foot view, education was the differentiator. But not just book smarts and credentials from accredited institutions. The outcomes that the education afforded created a significant fissure between success and more challenging paths.

I suggested that as a result of graduating from colleges or universities, we could gain access and exposure to white America in ways our contemporaries could not. We worked in corporate jobs and learned their mannerisms. Their speech patterns, colloquialisms, and jargon became our own. We learned to navigate white spaces in ways that would reduce the perception of otherness to the point of acceptability. Our educations served as the key to unlocking happy hours, weekend cookouts, golf outings, and cigar nights. It was the pathway that led us further from Blackness and closer to whiteness. In and of itself, the "Advantage" my father spoke of was associated with social mobility, which ultimately meant shedding the outward-facing mannerisms of uneducated Black folks, which increased fear amongst white people.

Disadvantaged meant having little to no interactions with white people that would require a significant shedding. If you didn't have to alter who you were, you could remain comfortable in your own neighborhoods, in your own social circles, and even more, in your own skin. But, you would be denied the opportunity to move up in social standing in the white world unless you, by some chance, were a star athlete or entertainer of some sort. We've seen countless football or basketball players plucked from inner cities or rural football factory towns and overnight thrust into a world of multi-million dollar contracts and immediate access to the world behind the veil: large luxury homes, exotic sports cars, endorsement deals, entourages, and beautiful women. Only to have it all wiped away the moment they blow out a knee or get into legal trouble due to their unwavering connection to their past lives. And within two to three years of leaving their professional sports careers behind, they find themselves broke and filing for bankruptcy. This is the price of being "Disadvantaged." They didn't spend time around white social norms, being privy to wealth management, investing, saving, or any financial literacy for that matter. They had to put their livelihoods in the hands of business managers or agents who don't operate in their best interests. People who have relationships with lawyers, accountants, and owners based on their inherent access and could position themselves to profit off of other people's labor. Disadvantaged meant being valuable and not valued, and this was only so long as your output was profitable and kept butts in seats.

I surmised that advantage was merely the ability to

reflect whiteness and thereby reduce the fear associated with being Black. Being disadvantaged meant being a staunch reminder of the effects of 450 years of systemic racism. That was a reminder that was certainly not welcome in broader white society, not in corporate spaces.

As an aside, we never actually answered the question that fueled the diner party. Who's responsible for dismantling systemic racism and how can it be achieved? Instead, we began at 6:00 PM and finished at 1:30 AM the next day and we couldn't get past the ground level topic of community.

You see, we collectively agreed and shared examples of how Black folks had found success in four out of five levels of Black self-sufficiency, as set forth by Dr. Claud Anderson in *Powernomics: The National Plan to Empower Black America*. For instance, we had economic success in that there were Black millionaires and billionaires. We had political successes in that we'd had Black politicians since the earliest days of reconstruction all the way up to a Black president. We showed examples of success in media control by naming several of the Black-owned media companies such as Ebony, Jet, OWN, Essence, Tyler Perry Studios, and so on. We even agreed on the fact that we had education control dating back as far as 1854 where the first HBCU was founded and at present-day having over 107 HBCUs still in operation. However, the one thing we couldn't agree on was how any of those individualized successes matriculated to a communal benefit. It was one thing to showcase our excellence through the societal standards of success, but what did it all mean if as a collective, we were still relegated to the bottom of the social ladder. It's as if the benefits of integration would come at the cost of Black obligation to ourselves. We lacked a moral standard, ethics, values, and a code of conduct that would govern how we engaged with each other. We were not obligated to support each other's business endeavors by patronizing and vertically integrating our ventures to create a closed-loop of economic power. We no longer possessed the communal agreement that if your neighbor caught your child doing wrong, they were fully empowered to correct the behavior in your absence, which maintained a standard of character and commitment. We lacked a standard of respect and empathy for our brothers and sisters that would ensure that if one was lacking, the other would fill the gaps. The very foundations of communal obligation that made a once thriving Greenwood, Oklahoma, or as it's better known, Black Wall Street, possible, are but a distant memory. What I'm speaking of is not fantasy. The communal obligation existed at one point in the Black community when America was segregated by law, but it still exists today in the Jewish, Arab, Asian, and Hispanic communities of America. The reason why a Mexican immigrant can come to the United States and within one to two years be operating a sustainable landscaping business with several employees, is because of their obligation to themselves. The reason why a Korean immigrant can set up a market in the middle of a Black neighborhood without ever having to learn the English language is through a support system that values their collective economic power over individual success. The reason why Cubans in Miami's Little Havana will not allow a non-Cuban business to be erected in their section of the city is that they know if you allow others to supply your community's needs, the economic strength of your community is jeopardized as the dollar no longer circulates among its own people. For all of these reasons we see living examples of what a communal obligation looks like, but for some reason, we opt not to emulate. It's as if the programming is too strong to overcome. The lack of trust in one another, and the selfish desire to be successful by any means necessary acts as an albatross that strangles our ability to be truly free.

I've had many conversations like this since the night of the dinner. I've asked many intelligent Black counterparts what it would be like to have a fresh start at building a Black community. If we could draft our own community standards, similar to a Homeowners Association community guideline that would govern the conduct of our community members, how would it look? Who would be allowed into the community and what would be the requirements for them to maintain membership? How would we enforce the rules and what would be the punishments or consequences for not adhering to the guidelines? How would the community architecture look? Would there be a Black architectural aesthetic that would signify to all who arrived at the community's thresholds that they were now entering a community of Black excellence? How would we govern the business and political affairs of the community? What measures would be in place to ensure we do not emulate a euro-colonized society? What would the education standards be and how would we leverage that education to further our ideals and aspirations? How would we replicate our values through the media to reinforce our culture and standards of normative behavior? All of these questions have served as a conversation starter, but I've often found myself with more insight into the problem rather than the solutions.

The most common theme I see when engaged in these conversations is the lack of creative thinking about what could be. Instead, the conversation usually devolves into dissertations on what is or has been and the possibility of what could be is hidden behind a curtain of historic trauma. We're married to the narrative of subjugation so much that when afforded an opportunity to imagine what freedom would feel like, it's quickly snapped back into reality like an involuntary reflex. I encourage people to approach these questions as if there were no constraints on possibilities and instead, they revert to the comfort of their current realities. I believe once we can freely co-create the solution without the constraints of conditioned thought, we may have a chance at laying the foundation of a Black community and thus a pathway to self-sufficiency.

Chapter Two

REPRESENTATION:
I DON'T SEE MYSELF HERE

It's September, and I'm landing at L.A.X. for the first time. I'm looking forward to a week of learning, networking, and discovery at one of the country's largest conferences, hosted by the largest professional social network company in the world, at the Anaheim Convention Center. Sure, I've attended conferences before, but this one was somehow different. I had accumulated a notable level of distinction as a thought leader in the space of Employer Brand and Recruitment Marketing, having helped build a global brand for one of the largest Pharma companies in the world. But that's not why this conference session was different. When I landed, I knew I would be receiving a phone call that could change my life. A call that would move my career forward as well as relocate my family. At that moment, the captain comes over the loudspeaker.

"Ladies and gentlemen, we're about fifteen minutes from our destination." He informs the flight attendants to prepare the cabin for landing. I haven't been this excited to land since I was a child on my first plane ride.

After what seemed like a lifetime, we landed. I got my luggage, headed to the hotel, and then it happened. My phone rang. It was the recruiter that I had become best friends with throughout my candidacy. She informed me that the offer letter should be in my inbox and if I had any questions, to give her a call.

"Congratulations and welcome aboard," she said. As soon as the call ended, I called my wife to tell her the great news. I think I said something like, "So are you ready to move to L.A.?" I confirmed I got the offer and everything would be in motion once I sent the signed offer letter back. She was so excited for me, for us.

The next few weeks were a blur, but I remember something that happened very early on in relocating my family from Chester County, PA, to Ventura County, CA. As we were researching real estate and ideal neighborhoods, my wife noticed something alarming. She looked up the demographic data of the location and it read as follows:

The racial makeup of Thousand Oaks is 101,702 (80.3%) White, 1,674 (1.3%) African American, 497 (0.4%) Native American, 11,043 (8.7%) Asian, 146 (0.1%) Pacific Islander, 6,869 (5.4%) from other races, and 4,752 (3.8%) from two or more races. Hispanic or Latino of any race were 21,341 persons (16.8%).

Having grown up in West Philadelphia and never living outside of P.A., my wife was extremely concerned. She was unsure of what it would feel like to live in a place where she may or may not see Black faces daily. She was afraid for our children, who would potentially be ridiculed or made to feel like they are less than because of their Blackness. It was something I never even considered or gave a thought to. Growing up in the suburbs all my life due to my parent's success in corporate America, I was used to being one of only a handful of Black people in my school and one of the only in my neighborhood. I knew the higher the income, the less likely it would be to see faces that resembled mine. I was fully prepared for this reality, having been one of six Blacks in my high school out of 2000 students. Being around so many white people without immediate access to Black culture brought a deep sense of anxiety to my wife, but off we went.

As part of my relocation package, the company provided a one-year membership in a transition group for newly relocated employees and their families. It was extremely beneficial for us as we were new to the area, and it allowed us to meet other new families who were new to both the company and the area. It also gave us some exposure to various activities in the community. Immediately, we recognized that most of the families in the group were of white or Asian descent. A few months later, a bi-racial family joined the group, and then an African family joined. It wasn't until our very last event after a year had transpired that we met two more Black families. In one year, we only met six new Black people in this group.

A few months into our new journey, my wife landed a job at the same company. Fortunately, we were able to forge some great relationships through being on campus daily. Before I paint a rosy picture for you, let me be clear. The only Black faces I would see on campus were those meandering to their next meeting, about the courtyards and campus grounds. Almost always, we would encounter one another in passing, and our gazes would connect. Then, in a universally understood head nod, we would acknowledge each other's uniqueness and excellence in solidarity. We were so scarce on the campus of our headquarters, which housed nearly 8,000 people, that when a new Black employee started, we would be able to recognize them immediately. Sadly, we were rarely together in meetings.

The reality for most of us is that we're the only ones who look like us in team meetings and on video conference calls. We spend most of our days isolated from each other, left to sneak moments to connect in between meetings or over lunch hours. And don't let us see a few Black colleagues that we know, in the courtyard, and gather in a group of two or more of us.

That's what we jokingly call, "A flag on the play." You see, just after the Civil War, America enacted the "Black Codes." One of those codes was the vagrancy law, which forbade freed Blacks from assembling in groups in the day or the night. Here's an example of the vagrancy law:

Section 2. Be it further enacted, that all freedmen, free Negroes, and mulattoes in this state over the age of eighteen years found on the second Monday in January 1866, or thereafter, with no lawful employment or business, or found unlawfully assembling themselves together either in the day - or nighttime, and all white persons so assembling with freedmen, free Negroes, or mulattoes, or usually associating with freedmen, free Negroes, or mulattoes on terms of equality, or living in adultery or fornication with a freedwoman, free Negro, or mulatto, shall be deemed vagrants; and, on conviction thereof, shall be fined in the sum of not exceeding, in the case of a freedman, free Negro, or mulatto, $150, and a white man, $200, and imprisoned at the discretion of the court, the free Negro not exceeding ten days, and the white man not exceeding six months.

(black code | Laws, History, & Examples | Britannica.
https://www.britannica.com/topic/black-code)

Essentially, if you had time to gather in a group, you must not have a job, and therefore, you'd be deemed a criminal. This plight befell so many Blacks in post-slavery America that its effects still resonate with today's modern Black folks' behaviors.

Seeing that there were enough of us around campus, I knew there had to be a better way to meet each other more readily. I had to find the plug for culture.

The first thing I did once I got access to my computer was to find the affinity group for Black employees. Having done a lot of work in the Diversity, Equity & Inclusion (DEI) space, I knew it would be my all-access pass to the Black community on campus. I signed up to gain membership and attended my first meeting a few weeks later. May I just say that being in a room with thirty other Black folks when you're typically not in a meeting room with even one evokes a feeling I struggle to articulate. The closest example I can provide to give a visual to this feeling is when Julie Andrews is singing in the alps that the hills are alive with the sound of music. Or better yet, how Ceilie felt when Nettie returned from Africa with her children, and they ran across the field to embrace each other. Those reading this and who haven't seen *The Color Purple*, take the opportunity to put this book down and watch it immediately. This film will up your credibility by at least 38% and qualify you to receive your "Black Card."

I felt the embrace instantaneously. I met many new

people who looked like me and sounded like me when I'm in familiar company. I listened to their job titles and the scope and scale of their work as everyone introduced themselves. I felt the full immersion in what we know as "Black excellence." For the first time in weeks, I was able to breathe. I could remove the mask and altered voice. I could unload the burden of suppressing my ethnicity. Amongst my fellow Black colleagues, there was no perceived threat, no stereotype, or labels. Finally, if only for the duration of this one-hour monthly meeting, I could be Black and relax.

Chapter Three

OPPORTUNITY NEVER KNOCKS: QUALIFIED BUT NOT CONSIDERED

I found myself in a deep and enthralling conversation about race and other Black people dynamics in America, with a White male executive at my company. This particular conversation was a carryover from a book club discussion we were participating in that covered the first few chapters of *White Fragility: Why It's So Hard for White People to Talk About Racism* by Robin DiAngelo. When it was time for Q&A in an open forum discussion format, he'd brought up the concept of meritocracy and the assertion that one's destiny is determined by their work ethic and grit. The discussion's moderator provided a polite answer that covered the surface level points, but I knew a more in-depth answer was in order.

I can't remember the exact words I used, but I know I ended the bold proclamation with "I reject the premise." He responded with a simple, "I understand," but having had a few deep conversations with him before, I knew that was simply an exit ramp to avoid an uncomfortable dialogue in a public forum. You see, this was no ordinary White male executive. In prior conversations, while traveling on business to one of our other sites, he shared with me that he grew up poor. He spent more time at his Black friend's house than he did his own. This exposure allowed him to see how we spoke when we weren't around other White folks. He got a front-row seat to watch our mannerisms, our inflections, our disdain for vanilla, and the insinuations that we would prefer to lead White lives. He got the unapologetic version of Blackness that didn't come through tv shows like *The Jeffersons* or *Sanford & Son*. So I knew there was a polar ice shelf beneath the waters in his agreeable answer. After the meeting ended, he sent me a text asking if we could put some time on the calendar to connect further on the subject.

We had forty-five minutes on the calendar when the call began. It was a video call, which I appreciated because it's always nice to see people's body language when discussing tough topics. We got through the pleasantries and got to the honest Q&A that we'd both come expecting. He first wanted to know my background. How did I come up, where had I lived, and what did my parents do for a living. I shared that I'd lived all across the country due to my parent's divorce when I was five and their successful pursuits in their careers. I provided my educational background as one of the only Black kids in the class for most of my life as a suburban resident. I juxtaposed that with the five years of experience living as the majority while attending an HBCU. I shared with him that my degree in African Studies helped me shed the despair that comes with knowing the contributions of African Black history before the transatlantic slave trade and seeing it all disappear because of colonization, at the age of nineteen. I think I provided a thorough understanding of how I view the world in a brief summation. He kindly thanked me for sharing this, and we dug in.

He wanted to revisit the conversation about meritocracy and my response because he felt it didn't adequately factor in data's intricacies on the subject. He suggested that Blacks' often leveraged position of not having a fair shake and that they weren't able to advance because of a systemic infrastructure designed to oppress them was not a viable argument. He asked me to react to that. I suggested that rugged individualism is a European concept that asserts that a person's destiny can be shaped by their willingness to work hard despite the perceived barriers. It implies that Black folks are lazy and unwilling to accept responsibility for their outcomes. It ignores the 450 years of hard, back-breaking work. I shared with him that a slave burial ground was unearthed on Wall Street in New York City. After forensic examinations of the bones, they found injuries on the large framed male skeletons that showed that muscles had detached from the bones due to overexertion. These injuries don't occur in the workplace any longer because no one works to this intensity level. I reminded him that all of this work was done for free and helped erect the wealthy institutions that, in some cases, still exist today. So no, I don't believe that meritocracy is real when you have an entire group of people who the law deemed slaves for eternity and never received credit for their work.

I further showcased how this lack of acknowledgment from hard work and how advancement opportunities fail to translate into reality in the modern workplace. I shared several stories with him of Black employees who had worked at the company for several years and had never received a promotion, despite their performance reviews being above expectations. We continued to explore a multitude of topics throughout the conversation, and by the time we wrapped up, we agreed that this would be the first of many more.

His thinking is consistently echoed by many white folks with similar ideas on various social media platforms. This notion that Blacks should stop complaining because they have the same opportunities as everyone else, and if they're not successful, then it's because they're not working hard enough. If only they could conceive a world through the lens of Black people.

I once spoke to a Black female colleague to expand my network at the company I had joined a few months earlier. As previously stated, I always make it a point to connect with Black folks where I work. *Nothing* beats a vast network. She was visiting headquarters and had several meetings, but based on my name's exposure because of the branding work I was doing for the company, she wanted to get time for us to meet. We exchanged our pleasantries and sat down in the conference room to begin our conversation. I pride myself on putting people at ease and shed the hierarchical constraints of titles. When I connect, I make it a safe space where we can connect authentically. This approach set the tone, which immediately led to putting her at ease as she began to open up. She proceeded to share that she was struggling to navigate a challenging situation with her boss. She consistently delivered on her objectives and produced work at a high standard. Still, she couldn't seem to go beyond a meets expectation on her performance reviews, and this was anchoring her in a position that was clearly beneath her potential.

Her manager was an African immigrant who came to the U.S. to attend college. His views of American Blacks was that of many Africans. Being a consumer of exported American culture, which provides a very skewed view of American Blacks especially, he saw us depicted as lazy squanderers of abundant opportunity. People who would buy gold chains at the moment of coming into any real money, luxury fashions, and expensive cars. This neatly packaged lie was the result of hip-hop culture becoming the number one export of America. Unfortunate as it may seem, this view profoundly shaped his perceptions of those of us he interacted with, and sadly, those who reported to him, which happened to include my colleague.

She also shared how one time in a coaching session, her manager advised that she should not expect anything more than a "meets expectations" on her performance review as that's all she's going to get from him. This exchange was six months before it was even time to consider the end of year performance ratings. She filed complaints to the staff relations team, but the claims went nowhere as she was not taken seriously by the investigator. Fortunately, an opportunity opened up in the department. She transferred to a different team where she received a promotion and found herself in a seemingly better situation, but it wouldn't last long.

It took someone seeing the value of what she brings to the table and making something happen. She was capable of so much more, but being overlooked and discounted from the very start was a reality all too familiar for Black women in corporate America.

I said, "Seemingly better" because not even a year in this new position did she start to experience even worse treatment. Her new boss was new to the company and was hired during the pandemic. She had never met her manager in person, so all of their interactions were through video conference calls. She noticed how every time they would meet for their one on ones, he paid her little attention. He would answer emails and seemed distracted while she talked. He would then ask her to repeat herself because he wasn't listening. He would also end the meetings after about fifteen to twenty mins into a thirty-minute session which also left her feeling undervalued. When she finally brought these behaviors up to her manager, he would respond with something so shocking that I was left speechless when she shared it with me. He confided in her that he was brought up to be racist towards Black people, and this is who he was. My colleague was just as speechless for a moment, but at least she now knew what type of person she was dealing with. Shortly after he shared this revelation, he abruptly ended the call.

This encounter prompted my colleague to go through all the proper procedures as one might expect after learning that your manager is a blatant racist. She informed human resources, her boss's boss, and even took it up the chain to the executive level. As a result, she experienced nothing short of typical for Black folks in corporate spaces. The employee relations team tasked with investigating employee complaints interrogated her as if she were the aggressor. Human Resources suggested she find a new boss to work for and get on a different team. The pleas to the executive level were met by kicking the issue back down the stairs to the boss's boss, who quickly enacted an apology campaign. They assured her they would give this particular manager "Coaching on how to be a better communicator," but no meaningful changes would ensue. She witnessed this organization fold itself into a pretzel trying to appease her rather than addressing their middle-manager layer's toxicity and remove the problem. Her only recourse was to seek legal counsel and proceed with a lawsuit. Again, this is nothing short of typical for Black folks in corporate spaces, unfortunately. What should have happened was this manager should have been written up. This should have been treated as a poor performance event and the manager should have been placed on an anti-racist improvement plan (ARIP). This plan would include required activities such as:

- *Mandatory unconscious bias training*
- *Reading of selected anti-racist books*
- *A community service project in an underrepresented community*
- *A 360-feedback review at the conclusion of the ARIP which includes the aggrieved and the offender's management team*

The measurement of success would be based on the assessment of the person who filed the complaint and whether they felt the offender has made a good faith effort to improve their behavior and that there have been noticeable changes in conduct. Examples of behavior change could be showcasing inclusive behaviors during meetings, being more attentive in 1:1 meetings and eliminating the dismissive behaviors, and a general reduction of the toxic micro-aggressive email communications and verbal exchanges. Based on these outcomes of the assessment and the 360-feedback evaluation, the offending manager would either have the ARIP removed or if no positive improvement was noted, they would be terminated. This would help to set a strong example for other would-be offenders that this type of behavior is antithetical to the inclusive culture the company seeks to create and maintain.

In a similar scenario, I was introduced to a young Black woman early in her human resources career. For purposes of anonymity and protection, we'll call her "Shonda." Having earned her master's degree in Human Resources from a prominent program in the midwest, she had joined the company as part of a leadership development program. This program would enable her to rotate through several functions within HR, giving her exposure to multiple business elements and increasing her acumen, and broadening her professional skillset at an accelerated pace. She hailed from the South Side of Chicago and had a fiery midwest accent that told a story with every inflection.

She was strong, resilient, and determined to achieve success. I immediately saw a brilliant light in this young woman and made it a point to serve as an informal mentor.

One day I got a call from my young Chi-town mentee and could feel the urgency over the phone. She shared that her final rotation was coming to an end in a few months, and she wasn't sure if she'd be considered for a full-time role once the program was over. Based on all the anecdotal feedback I'd received from colleagues who'd interacted with her, I thought she was being a bit hard on herself, as, indeed, the company would find a place for this rising star. She suggested that the other people in her cohort had received invites from HR leadership to discuss opportunities coming up and wanted to start evaluating options for them after the program concluded. What she told me next was heart breaking.

She recalled how the first of her three rotations was at headquarters in the Talent Acquisition function. At the time, her manager was an Indian gentleman who showed very little interest in developing her career. She told me that on several occasions, he would talk down to her as if she were incapable of understanding basic instructions. When the incidents became too obvious to ignore, she filed a complaint with staff relations. She reported the behaviors that seemed to be discriminatory and awaited further guidance through the proper channels. About a week later, in a one on one meeting, her manager told her, "You don't go to HR on me. I tell you how this works, and if you don't like it, you come to me. Never go to HR on me." This retaliatory behavior from a mid-level manager is unacceptable, but what recourse is she left with? Fortunately, this manager was fired a few months later, and the situation got brushed under the rug.

Her second assignment was a combination of the development program manager trying to correct the first rotation's wrongs and figuring out where to fit her. They presented an opportunity to work on a new project that had historically not gotten off the ground due to a lack of sponsorship. Granted, this project wasn't necessarily in the wheelhouse of her skillset, but it would be an excellent visibility play and could increase her viability at the company if successful. If you think this sounds like a set up for failure, you're right.

As I write this, companies are vigorously searching for Black talent. In some cases, they want to appear as if they address low representation problems, while others are taking actions simply to avoid looking tone-deaf. The more significant issue here is that they are not looking at the wealth of internal talent they already employ. When you open the flood gates for external talent to pour in, the signal you're sending to your existing employees is that you don't see the value in those who already know your culture, business practices, and processes. You are devaluing their contributions to your bottom line and overlooking the leadership potential waiting to rise from within your ranks. Granted, you need to increase the representation. Full stop. However, you also have to walk and chew gum at the same time. A good friend who made it to a Director role after seventeen years with the company wrote a letter to Corporate America. I share this with you because her experiences are a universal reflection of Black professional women whose brilliance is dimmed by ineptitude seated in leadership positions.

Dear Corporate America,

I would like to offer you my resignation. Although it may come to you as a surprise, I have been weighing the pros and cons of my decision for several years. I've reached a point in my career where it's time to part ways. By all means, please do not misunderstand my intentions. I plan to remain employed by you and continue to passionately bring medicines to patients and deliver to your bottom line.

However, I am <u>resigned</u> to hold you accountable for the persistent and underlying systemic racism that impedes my full potential. To be fair, I appreciate that you may *be unaware of how you have played a role in my decision to resign. I have outlined three key actions below that we need to take to make progress. But first, it's important to provide some upfront context for additional alignment.*

I have been working side by side with you for 25 years. I have checked every box and have made it here as your colleague, acquaintance, and likely only Black friend. I graduated top of my class in both high school and undergrad. I earned a 4-year degree in Finance from a highly reputable HBCU and secured my first job at a top tier investment bank. I competed with the best and brightest to earn a spot at the most prestigious entry-level management program offered by Wall Street. My fellow new hires were Harvard, Boston University, Stanford, Cornell, and Brown graduates from all over the country, and they were wicked smart, just like me. Following my stint on Wall Street, I attended the University of Chicago (a consistently top 5 MBA program) and earned an MBA with a concentration in Finance and Economics.

I married my high school sweetheart, and we have two beautiful children, ages 15 and 4. No, I did not grow up "in the hood." But I was raised in a predominantly Black working-class neighborhood on a quiet cul de sac. Our neighborhood was comprised of mostly two-parent homes. My brother's 5th-grade teacher lived around the corner, so he was always on his best behavior when she was in her yard. Our neighborhood only had one Asian family that recently immigrated to America. They didn't stick around very long. The rumor was that the kid's dad got a new job, and the family moved to the other side of town, the "better" side. Other than a few fistfights between neighborhood kids, our lives were ordinary. No drive-by shootings, no police raids, and no memorable stories about how violence has impacted my life and my ability to overcome the unimaginable horrors of growing up Black. Sorry, that's not my story.

I was bussed to school 25 minutes away for a "better" education. My friends were on the bus, and we passed a neighborhood school on the way.

None of us ever questioned why half of the neighborhood kids went on the bus, and the other half walked to school. We just knew our school was "better" because it was on the "good" side of town where my future husband lived. I'm thankful for being bussed because it expanded my horizons and opportunities. As an added benefit, I met my best friend, who I married 20 years later. The lack of traumatic events in my early life did not make me less interesting in my formative years. It was quite the opposite. I was a student leader, a cheerleader in high school and college, and I dabbled in university politics. By my third year, I ascended to the role of Miss Junior. I enjoy leading others and have a drive and passion for making situations better. I had what it takes to conquer the world — goals, drive, ambition, and education to prove it. Then I met you, Corporate America. I quickly realized that the new game I was entering had different rules, and I was woefully unprepared.

See Me

Today I am a full-time working mom with no illusions of having it all. I play to win and compete hard, but my presence at work is obscured. It's obscured because I was told this is what is needed to make it in your world. Don't be too outspoken, don't ask clarifying questions, always smile, blah, blah blah. Early in my career, I received feedback from a white leader that I was too analytical and needed to focus more on the softer skills to be successful.

She said my quickness and sharp wit made others feel inadequate. Another manager told me I needed to direct my attention to observing my environment and listening more. Basically, he was saying just shut up and do the work! Instead of helping me refine and leverage my strengths, both of these leaders focused on my gaps and belittled my authentic style.

I seek joy in my work and personal life while encouraging the same for my family and direct reports. I focus my team's success on trust, empowerment, and flexibility to deliver results. Everyone knows this alone will not unleash full potential. Networking, political savvy, and storytelling are essential parts of the formula to success in any environment. I've played this game before, but something just hasn't clicked since I've arrived at your doorsteps, Corporate America.

Growing up Black, I was not given the key to unlocking the white network either professionally or socially. When I was first promoted to sales leadership, I reached out to two white female peers from my small team to assist with interviewing candidates for an opening on my new team. I called both women independently (twice!), only to be left with no response from either colleague. I knew then that I would not be welcomed to the leadership team with open arms. Who knew that my expectations were too high to assume that these colleagues with years of hiring experience would lend a helping hand with screening my first direct report hire. My expectations were further lowered in a social setting with team members. While I'm accustomed to being excluded from your weekend socializing, it hit me pretty hard when a colleague invited my direct reports and excluded me and the one other Black female in the Region from her baby shower. When I expressed to my colleague that my feelings were hurt, she dismissed me by saying my presence would have made things awkward, and it was easier this way. Easier to have a party with white work colleagues.

Everyone knows that networking can unlock potential and open doors to the executive suite. Being a Black woman, I'm expected to play by a different set of rules that keep the doors slammed shut. I have focused on working smart, solving problems, promoting others, and developing solutions to improve our patients' lives. If only Corporate America would have offered me a key. See me in your network. See me as a trusted teammate. See me as a leader in your organization.

Hear Me

I have something to say, and I want to be heard. I want colleagues to acknowledge my contributions, not reiterate what I just communicated or, worse yet, repackage it and sell it as their idea. I want allies to stop saying, "I believe what she is trying to say is…." I want leaders to stop shutting me down and ignoring what I have to say because my title is not as high as others in the room, even though I have developed significant expertise across various functional areas within the organization. I hear you when it's implied that I need to "know my place." I don't hear you saying that I have potential, and you trust me to continue to lead with conviction in whatever role I occupy.

Hear me when I share a personnel issue during calibration, and my integrity is challenged in front of the all-White male leadership team. Obviously, there is truth to both sides of a story, wink, wink. I must be misreading the situation. The employee in question is an outstanding team player and contributor, and I got it wrong. Let's promote this person instead! Hear me when I inquire about a high-profile project that is critical to achieving our goals this year. It's too bad that I didn't speak up and make my interest known earlier. You had no idea I would be interested in such an amazing opportunity.

Hear me when I tell you the qualifications and reasons I deserve an upcoming open role, and you tell me that you'll have to stick your neck out with the hiring manager on my behalf. I should owe you my gratitude and loyalty for your support. Apparently, without your help, I would have never made it this far on talent alone.

When I pushback or challenge you, I'm not being defensive, nor am I being too aggressive. I simply disagree with you and seek to find a common, elegant solution that is thoughtful and nuanced. Hear me because I feel like screaming!

Free Me

Slavery ended in America almost 200 years ago, yet I remain shackled by the echoes of the oppression my ancestors endured. Progress has been eroded in the past 30 years alone. For the next generation, there is no longer bussing in my old neighborhood, and the schools have returned to being predominantly segregated. I'm a visionary, constantly seeking change to create a different reality. This attitude drives me to keep pushing the boundaries and fighting for equality. Freedom without the ability to reach my full potential is exhausting, both physically and mentally. Thank you, Corporate America, for inviting me to the party. I'm the Black woman standing in the corner with no offers to take a turn on the dance floor. Many terrible dancers are taking up space on the center-stage. It's now your time to showcase my moves, cheer me on, and free me to spin.

Please accept my letter of resignation to keep challenging the status quo.

I write it on behalf of all Black Americans working in Corporate America.

Regards,
Shonda

At the time of this writing, Shonda is still working in corporate America. However, she has begun to recognize that the abusive relationship she's in is untenable and is exploring what it would look like to truly control her own destiny. Whether that be through entrepreneurial endeavors or a better balance of her existing relationship with the company and her personal development.

THE FAILED PROMISE OF INTEGRATION

As of July 2020, there are only four Black CEOs in Fortune 500 ranked companies. Out of the four, zero are women. This sobering fact means that at best, we as Black people, only have a 0.6% chance of becoming the CEO of a major company, and that's if you're a Black man. According to a 2019 report by the Center for Talent Innovation, Blacks represented 13% of the U.S. population but only held 3.2% of senior leadership jobs at Fortune 500 companies. In this same study, about 65% of Blacks said they have to work harder to advance, as compared with only 16% of white employees. This data speaks to the adage that every Black person in the working world knows since very young ages—being Black means you have to work twice as hard for half the recognition.

I'm reminded of the time I was discussing my performance review with my manager. I had a stellar year. It was recognized with the generous bonus I received and the overwhelmingly positive sentiment my anonymous colleagues shared in my 360 feedback. When asked if I had any questions, I took the opportunity to bring up a promotion to Director. I'll never forget what my manager said in the presence of myself and a VP. My manager said that once you "flawlessly" deliver the Global Employer Brand, we can revisit that discussion. "Flawlessly?" I didn't know how to respond. As I walked out of that meeting, I had so many questions.

For instance, how could someone put a condition of flawless delivery on promotion opportunities? Besides, how would they know what flawless delivery looked like since they'd never developed or deployed a global brand before? I was baffled, frustrated, and left feeling like I had no one invested in my success. The other thing that stood out was how they used the money to subdue my desire for elevation in my title. This sort of thing happens far too often to talented Black employees. If you're compensated with bonuses and incentives, then you should be happy and shut up. However, those bonuses face tax rates of no less than 22%, and let's not forget that Blacks are paid $0.59 for every $1.00 of their white counterparts. So what then should we be doing differently? Suppose we perform at high levels and are assuaged with hefty lump-sum bonuses but are denied access to more senior titles and increased leadership opportunities. What are we left to think?

One of the things I struggle with internally is this feeling that we're fighting for the wrong things. Our struggle to integrate into mainstream society caused the demise of the Black community's self-sufficiency and collective strength. In today's struggle to reach the upper tiers of major companies, I can't help but feel like we're putting an exceeding amount of effort into running the plantation while crying indignant injustice to the masters for not allowing it. The truth is, these are White-owned companies with long-standing norms of Black leadership exclusion, whose successes do not benefit the Black community. Imagine what we could achieve if we took the collective talents of corporate America's most brilliant Black minds and funneled that expertise into self-sustaining Black businesses. The amount of innovation and excellence that's achievable is beyond measure. Just like the civil rights movements of the '50s and '60s, access to White society and structures is the end goal, possibly because it's something that had been out of reach for so long. Access to the c-suite is out of reach today, so we find ourselves vying for white managers to recognize our hard work and pull us up into the leader's seat when we should be looking for ways to validate ourselves by the standards we set for ourselves. I suggest there's a damning admission that's required by white execs. One that may be too hard to make without an honest realization. Maybe you just don't want us to lead. Or maybe there's an admission that we as Black people need to make, and it's that we're afraid to leave the plantation.

In 1866, The Lincoln Administration freed nearly 4.5 million Black Americans from bondage. This action released us into society with no means of sustaining a living. We had not been educated. We had nowhere to live, no job prospects, and no money. We were in a society where the competition for labor against white workers was a direct threat to our very lives, let alone livelihoods. Without question, leaving a life of servitude for one of freedom is immensely better than remaining in bondage without hope. However, suppose you are not prepared to embrace a life of freedom and the responsibilities that come along with it. In that case, your most inevitable recourse is a return to that which you are most comfortable.

One-fourth of newly freed Black folks died due to starvation and disease. A smaller amount found ways to sustain a new life of freedom by migrating across the country and up to Canada. However, the majority returned to the plantations that they were recently emancipated from and did so for a wage that was so low, they were nearly indistinguishable from slaves once again. While the laws of the land expressly forbade chattel slavery, the evolved institution of sharecropping had taken its predecessor's place. In a system of inherent indebtedness to the farm owner, the Black worker would always find themselves in arrears at the end of the year. Even worse would be the ever-moving goalposts of success. If you were contracted to produce X amount of farmed goods by the end of the year, nothing was stopping the landowner from saying that you were actually supposed to have Y amount, and now you owe them more sweat to make up for the deficit.

These were the realities of those who chose to go back to the lives they, and nearly ten generations of family before them, knew. The ones who opted to play their hand at freedom to make a go of it on their own suffered immensely more. The truth is that even the non-slaveholding northern states were no friends of the newly freed Blacks. Many faced ill-treatment from Union soldiers, while others found it nearly impossible to secure meaningful work to feed themselves or their families. White proprietors would rather see white men employed than to give much-needed jobs to Black people. For those that did navigate their way to sustainable living in other parts of the country, it was still no walk in the park. Some moved to Canada to start anew, while others moved to northern cities and western boomtowns.

The best examples we have are Black communities like Rosewood in Florida or Greenwood in Tulsa, Oklahoma. If you know history, just hearing those two names should spark a wave of fear and concern. The best example of what happens when Blacks folks thrived in a post-slavery scenario was Greenwood, also known as "Black Wall Street." This thriving town was the epitome of Black success in the early 1900s. You had Black-owned banks, grocery stores, tailors, lawyers, and mechanics. The dollar bounced many times over within the community, creating a comfortable living for many middle and upper-middle-class families. The only problem was that the community thrived well beyond the living standards that the surrounding white communities experienced. As a result of their jealousy and outrage, in 1921, the town was set ablaze. To date, Tulsa is one of the worst examples of domestic terrorism in American history. Nearly 300 Blacks were killed, and the entire town was burned to the ground.

Greenwood's cautionary tale is used to show Black folks what happens when you entertain ideas of becoming self-sufficient. Even more so, the narrative of doing as well as or surpassing their white counterparts is ill-advised for the potential repercussions that come with your success. I believe we as Black folks are afraid of branching off on our own because of stories like this. Interestingly, we haven't seen another Greenwood since in America.

It's for these reasons that Black advancement in corporate spaces becomes a tedious tightrope walk. You want to showcase your talents and aptitude for success, however, doing so comes with consequences. Sure, we could always find another job at another company where we'd be offered more money and perhaps, a higher title. But the reality is, we'd be trading one plantation shingle for another. When you have bills, children, health challenges, and debt, it's tough to think about anything other than a stable and guaranteed income. This plight has become the modern-day dilemma that our ancestors faced when they were newly freed and venturing out past the plantations' thresholds they'd always known. We have a decision to make as a collective, and that is, will the Black workforce of tomorrow remain chained to the concepts of success that were sold to our ancestors? Or will we decide there's another construct we can create for ourselves that doesn't rely on waiting for White validation? When you graduate from high school, you go to a predominantly white college or university, graduate and get a good-paying job, work for thirty years, and then retire. If this model sounds archaic to you as you read it, you're not alone. This narrative may have fit the model of the 1950's post-world war II era middle class American dream, but even that dream didn't include Black people. In 2020, we found ourselves to be some of the highest educated and most qualified, yet we have not realized that our qualifications are no surrogate for the entitlements afforded our white counterparts. The amount of effort, energy, and collective brilliance that could be applied to building our own companies continues to be given away to companies that are still trying to figure out how to see us at all.

The failed promise of integration was that we assumed it would mean inclusion and equality. Integration simply meant we would gain access to white institutions but weren't promised advancement opportunities. We were afforded the right to patronize white establishments, but it didn't mean we'd be able to afford the food nor did it ensure quality service. Integration has meant the implicit requirement that we assimilate into white environments so as not to cause any disruptions to the status quo. Any attempt at calling out the incompatibility of integration and the maintenance of one's own culture is met with swift opposition. Corporate America has been wrestling with this notion for over five decades. The outward exclamation that we must celebrate the differences in our workforce has been countered by the unspoken truth that celebration doesn't connote elevation. If we intend to address the failures of diversity and inclusion within the workplace then we must first examine the underlying notion that non-white employees must conform to a white standard.

WELCOME TO THE BURNING BUILDING

I find myself offering a different proposition to young Black HBCU students nearing their graduation dates and looking to get into the workforce. To help them understand the road that lies ahead, I hit them with an unorthodox pitch. It goes a little something like this:

I work for company X, and we are hiring. We are looking for the cream of the Black crop talent who are hungry, ambitious, and willing to get paid $0.59 on the dollar vs. their white counterparts for the same job and twice the output. Some of the things you can expect in your everyday include being the only one that looks like you in meetings. The sense of isolation you'll feel by being the only Black member of your team or only seeing Black people in passing will be amplified when you notice that there are no Black leaders on the executive team. Your hard work and examples of Black excellence instilled in you during your time at [Insert HBCU here] will be overlooked, hi-jacked by your white counterparts, or blatantly rejected as overly ambitious grandstanding. Your excellence will shine a glaring spotlight on white mediocrity and, in fair exchange, will relegate you to a ceiling of middle management at best. At the end of the year, your stellar track record of delivering results and setting division records will be rewarded in your performance review. Your manager will advise you to be more of a team player and that you're still a few years away from a leadership position. Meanwhile, you'll see your white counterparts, and in some cases, those you've trained, be tapped for more prominent roles and promotions only by virtue of them showing up, being from a higher pedigree alma mater, or the personal relationships they have with leadership outside of work. You'll also enjoy the perks of microaggressive emails, passive-aggressive remarks in virtual meetings, and dismissive one on ones with your managers. The trade-offs for your sacrifice of psychological safety, dignity, and in some cases, your physical well-being, is a steady paycheck, a 401k, and health insurance. All of which will keep you tethered to the treadmill of false hope that one day you'll become the CEO. If all of this sounds like the ideal experience you've always dreamed of, please apply today.

While this may sound like the epitome of bitter pessimism, I can't stress enough how important it is to be upfront and honest with Black youth coming into the workforce. I want early career Black talent to walk into a corporate situation with their eyes wide open and no misgivings about the challenges that lie ahead. Most importantly, I want them to question the premise of why they're seeking a corporate job in the first place. Is it because this is what they want to do, or are they executing the American dream's well-encoded programming? The American capitalist construct was built on the notion of having a well-supplied labor class to support the industries and fortunes of the wealthy. This means that our K-12 education system is designed to pump out more employees than owners. Our financial system promotes debt by way of student loans, credit cards, mortgages, and car notes, which will require a good-paying job to pay the interest off at a slow drip pace. Our entertainment industries send the repeated signals of what success looks and feels like in contrast to our ordinary lives by showcasing luxury lifestyles, fame, and notoriety. All of these seemingly disconnected cogs are the well-oiled mechanical Turk that was designed to mislead the masses in an elaborate hoax that was branded "The American Dream."

Interestingly the misdirection was hidden in plain sight. It's called a dream for a reason. We were not given the exposure to self-sufficiency, entrepreneurialism, or leadership, but instead, we were shown how to obey, follow, and comply. Now imagine, if instead of spending four years in a higher institution of learning to attain a credential that gains us admission to the working class, we leveraged the knowledge we acquired to then apprentice at a company with the intent of building our own businesses. Interesting approach, right? We would trade time for money as part of a continuing curriculum of learning the industries' inner mechanics. We could build our networks to include close relationships with people in finance, supply chain, business development, sales, marketing, human resources, research and development, and customer service, all with the intent of one day partnering with these very people to establish our own conglomerates of vertically and horizontally aligned businesses. If only we had the mindset to approach work this way. Instead, as the descendants of those who returned to the plantations so many years ago, we settled for the failed promise of integration. Not realizing that diversity doesn't equate to inclusion and inclusion doesn't equate to belonging, and belonging doesn't equate to equity. The elaborate rouse that is integration has left us more segregated in some aspects than our forefathers in the pre-civil rights era. We've been allowed access to gaze at white reality in close proximity but not empowered to embrace that reality as our own. At least not without paying a significant price that leaves us culturally bankrupt and emotionally depleted.

Chapter Four

THE WORLD DOESN'T STOP WHEN YOU'RE AT WORK: CALLING IN BLACK

It's a Wednesday. Two days back at work after a long Memorial Day weekend. The upcoming Friday is another vacation day leading to another long weekend. But this week isn't like other weeks. Something is off. In two days, I've seen a woman weaponize her white tears in Central Park, and the same day, a Black man is killed by a police officer on video by way of a knee to the neck, leading to his death by suffocation. A few weeks prior, we witnessed three armed white men ambush a young Black man in a Georgia neighborhood and gun him down like hunted prey. It's only Wednesday, and I feel like a war veteran who's witnessed the atrocities of war. Yet to my white counterparts, it's just another Wednesday.

Far too often, seeing Black lynchings by law enforcement is the norm in my community but doesn't even make it to white neighborhoods' radars. It's as if we live on two different planets with different news cycles. I wonder if the lack of recognition comes from centuries of blocking Black visibility from view as part of public policy and entrenched etiquette within white communities or is it merely that epigenetics has left white people with an encoded incapability of feeling empathy for Black people based on codified cognitive dissonance? It is a dissonance required to justify four centuries of slavery and Jim Crow institutions.

I remember July 8, 2016. Much like the story above, we were coming back to the office after a long holiday weekend. Having just celebrated the independence of the country, which is bittersweet for Black folks. This day in the office was not unlike any other for my white counterparts. Most of them stopping by my cubicle and asking how my 4th was. Did I do anything or go anywhere? I feigned a smile and forced a surface-level answer because I just wasn't feeling it that particular day. Today, I could feel my Blackness so palpably that it was almost as if I could see myself as a third-party observer. Today, something was noticeably different. So much so that my boss could tell something was not quite right with me. I appreciated how my manager always made herself available and was candid with me during our conversation. She invited me into her office, and as we sat down, she asked what's wrong? I sunk back in the chair as if a therapist was questioning me. I unloaded.

I told her about a horrific video I saw the evening before. It was a Facebook live stream by a young Black woman in her car. Her boyfriend was in the passenger seat and their daughter was in the backseat. I remember the woman being so composed. The police had stopped them for a broken tail light. The officer was standing outside the passenger side window with his weapon drawn, screaming frantically in shock. The passenger was slumped over towards the center armrest with a blood-soaked white t-shirt. The woman on the driver's side was calmly stating facts to the officer. She recounted what happened and noted that the officer asked her boyfriend to produce his license and registration. The gentleman informed the officer that he was a licensed gun owner, and he did have the firearm in the vehicle. As the officer commanded the man to put his hands back where he could see, four shots rang out. He hit the man in the chest at point-blank range. As he lay slumped over and dying in front of his family, his girlfriend was reporting real-time to the live audience of what just happened. Clearly in shock, she repeated over and over, "Please don't tell me he's dead. Please don't tell me he went out like this." I finished the story of what I and by this time, hundreds of thousands of people had witnessed and remembered Gina's face being overwhelmed with horror. Her empathy was like a life raft in the middle of the Atlantic Ocean for me but only provided a moment of respite. All she could do was listen and empathize as best she could. The thing she asked me that I wasn't prepared for was if I needed to take the day off and return when

I was ready. I hadn't even considered this as a reason to take a day off. I had become so used to seeing these things and then coming in to work as if nothing happened. That recommendation meant everything.

> "Have you ever just wanted to call in Black? You realize something [...] another unarmed Black person was assaulted and or murdered. As I was driving into work with water pouring from my eyes, I realized something: I was grieving [...] Sometimes, I need a minute! And that's where calling in Black (would be so clutch. Oh no, it's not contagious, I just need a solid day to reaffirm my humanity to myself, so, see you tomorrow."
>
> - Evelyn From The Internets, 2015

There are long-lasting effects of having to cover our traumas in the workplace. This masquerade that we're forced to put on to remain employed and leave our humanity at the security desk when we badge in is not sustainable. In the first few weeks after the murder of George Floyd, my wife broke down. I mean literally broke down. She cried to the point of convulsion and felt so afraid, she locked herself in our bedroom closet. You would think with the outpouring of care, concern, and compassion from white colleagues, she would feel more supported than ever, but the opposite was true. She felt an acute awareness of her Blackness in a way that she had never felt before. White folks' outreach made her feel as if she was on display like Ota Benga, the Mbuti man known for being featured in an exhibit at the 1904 Louisiana Purchase Exhibition in St. Louis, Missouri, and later as a human zoo exhibit at the Bronx Zoo in 1906. It's worth mentioning that the depression he later fell into after being freed caused him to commit suicide just ten years later.

Her feelings of isolation in all-white meetings increased ten-fold. She was more aware of her codeswitching and the need to do it amid these uncomfortable conversations, just so white folks felt more at ease. No one prepares you to go from being mostly invisible to being thrust into the spotlight for all to revel in your naked vulnerability, insecurities, and ancestral trauma. Daily, we sat in open forum discussions, asked to share our intimate encounters with racial injustice, and moderate safe space Q&A's as if we weren't still processing the horrors of seeing a Black man get lynched on national television. Most of us felt the pain and silent cries of our ancestors coming out through us who had never been asked to share their pain so freely. We were exhausted.

This experience moved me to start writing. I created the "Allyship Series," a group of articles on LinkedIn and Medium that addressed the textures of the moment we found ourselves in as a Black collective. The following is one of those articles:

THE CONVERSATION I WASN'T
PREPARED FOR

This week I've had to have conversations I never thought I would in my lifetime. It wasn't the conversation with my nine-year-old son and my seven-year-old daughter that hurt the most. I knew I'd have to have that conversation at some point, but I thought I'd have more time. I had to explain to my son why police murdered George Floyd on film, and no one helped him. I had to demonstrate how he is to conduct himself if he is engaged by police and what to do with his hands at all times. I had to model how to respond in the most non-threatening ways possible and to follow instructions to the tee, or it could cost him his freedom, or worse, his life. No, this conversation, or "The talk" as we know it in the Black community, was inevitable. The conversation I was utterly unprepared for and having no reference frame to reach back on were the conversations I had with my white colleagues.

The calls I received from my white colleagues who were distraught by what happened and felt a sense of paralysis unearthed a theme that I've come to find out is common amongst many in their community. They couldn't imagine what I must be going through and wanted desperately to know how they could help, but this is a theme for another piece coming up in the series, so I'll park this one right here. The theme that was unearthed came from a series of calls I was invited to attend. These open forum dialogues were designed for leadership to make consoling remarks and then open up the line for the Black employees to share their thoughts, reactions, and stories. After several of these calls, I could run the script as if it were a well-written screenplay on the silver screen. I heard countless stories of racial injustice in the communities. Black men being pulled over and harassed by police in predominantly white neighborhoods. Black women being profiled or treated with a lack of respect or human decency while patronizing retail stores. The microaggressive behaviors by white managers in corporate settings, denials of promotions despite being the highest performers, the lower pay received for the same work. These and many more accounts left Black employees feeling less than human, and they were often the only Black employee in the room, department, or organization. Now imagine being on four to five of these calls a day for five days straight. These don't include the individual calls you find yourself on, having to relive these encounters as well.

Meanwhile, you still have a job to do and perform at the highest levels. To say that anyone would be exhausted daily would be the understatement of the century. Or better yet, several centuries.

Don't get me wrong, this is a necessary part of the process, and I believe we have to take time to be heard.

But let me share with you why this is so exhausting, and trust me, it's not for the reason you think.

Anyone would be exhausted from telling the same story every day on a loop. Still, it would be even more exhausting if you were doing so while dealing with the trauma of relived experiences of centuries worth of racial injustices. Add that Black people must show up to the workplace every day and put on the mask, which we affectionately know as "code-switching." This daily wardrobe enables us not to be deemed threatening, aggressive, loud, or overly ambitious, lest we are labeled by stereotypical depictions of Black unworthiness. We even have to do it during a time such as this. Something I don't think that has been realized yet by our white counterparts is the level of mental fortitude it takes to be Black in America, let alone corporate America, and I completely get it. This is yet another thing you will discover in the wake of George Floyd's murder, which will add to your cultural competency, and for that, I'm willing to push through the exhaustion.

The Stories We'd Never Heard Before

One of the things I've been encouraged by is hearing the stories of my white counterparts. Their experiences of being white and reflecting on times where they were witness to or unwitting participants in moments of racism were, in some ways, cathartic. To finally hear that they recognized the inhumanity and the shame they felt for being silent was something I had never seen before, except in the movies.

One woman shared with me that she grew up in a small town where there were virtually no Black people. She would hear racist commentary so regularly while at school or in the community, it was only a matter of time before these thoughts became her own. She went on to tell me something she hadn't shared with anyone besides her husband. When she was nine years old, she repeated a racial epithet in her household that was so vile, her father slapped her across the face. He immediately scolded her for using such disgusting language and let her know it was not something he tolerated in his household. To this day, she has never forgotten that experience.

Another colleague who grew up in the deep south reflected on having a Black friend back in high school, whom they had to sneak into their trailer park to hang out. They would do so by having one white friend on either side of their Black friend in the car's back seat. The Black friend would sink down low in the seat so as not to be seen. They'd hang out and listen to music, drink, and talk until it was time to go home. They'd repeat the cloak and dagger operation of getting him out of the trailer park at the end of the night to not be caught. The consequences of being discovered would have been dire, to say the least.

Hearing these stories has been by far more impactful for me than the sharing of my own, and it's something I think will need to continue if we want to get to a place of healing and reconciliation. The truth is that Black people have 450 years of stories that can be shared. You even have academy award-winning films, documentaries, music, and best-selling books that capture the pain, joys, perseverance, humanity, and inhumanity of our collective experiences as Black Americans. A willingness to seek them out and the desire to put the time in to absorb them is something you'll need to decide is a worthy endeavor. We have told our stories for so long and often as a cry for help or a plea for recognition and validation by the white community that to do so now seems tiring at best. Our stories were the flashlights in the darkness that reminded us that we mattered and showed you the same. Now and only now are these stories receiving the audience we've sought for generations.

I find myself energized amid exhaustion by this unique moment in history and will continue to do my part to voice our stories and yours. My deepest hope is that this moment lasts beyond the headlines. I hope it lives longer than the initiatives and public statements of silence no more. I hope this awakening turns the page for a story that has yet to be told in this country. Fortunately, we're writing it as co-authors, together for the first time in American history.

Visual Resources for Allies:

For those looking to hear some of our stories for the first time or revisit some you've heard before, I offer these resources. A fellow global employer brand luminary at Netflix® shared a playlist of films and documentaries that can help provide perspective on the Black experience. While these by no means are the whole of our experiences, they are a great starting point while you have downtime. Also, I'm including some of the most eye-opening lectures from voices who have been doing ground-breaking work to lift the veil on white supremacy and systemic racism. I hope you find these to be timely aides on your continued journey towards newfound enlightenment and allyship.

Post Traumatic Slave Disorder by Dr. Joy DeGruy Leary
https://www.youtube.com/watch?v=BGjSday7f_8

White Privilege, Racism, White Denial & The Cost of Inequality by Tim Wise
https://www.youtube.com/watch?v=uPiGMP-_B3I

White Rage: The Unspoken Truth of Our Nation's Divide
https://www.youtube.com/watch?v=YBYUET24K1c

Dr. Robin DiAngelo discusses *White Fragility*.
https://www.youtube.com/watch?v=45ey4jgoxeU

Jane Elliot: Blue Eye Brown Eye Experiment
https://www.youtube.com/watch?v=jPZEJHJPwIw

Jacob Blake's shooting was the next riot inducing expression of police aggression and lack of humanity displayed for all to see across social media. He was shot seven times in the back at close range. I don't mean close range in the sense that there was a small number of feet between him and Blake. I mean close range in that the officer was holding Blake's shirt in his left hand while firing seven shots with his right hand. All of this is in full display of Jacob's eight-year-old son sitting in the back seat of the SUV. Having to witness this traumatic experience in person is unconscionable, but seeing it via social media was no less traumatic. As per usual, after I saw another tragic shooting of someone that looked like me, I had to carry on to work. This shooting was almost three months to the day since George Floyd's murder, and the country had not yet fully healed. One would think the level of outrage, public outcry, and glaring spotlight on social injustice would have been a deterrent for law enforcement. But that would assume that killing unarmed Black people is enough to move white folks to empathy and sweeping change. Unfortunately, history is the cruelest teacher on the subject.

As I sat in a meeting late Tuesday after the shooting, I noticed my colleagues were in a particularly jovial mood. One of my counterparts was taking the call from his car while on the way to Santa Barbara. He placed his phone in the cup holder near his armrest and angled the camera so viewers were looking up at him. One of my other counterparts, an early forty-something white woman from Ohio, calls out that he looks like he's a police officer ready to jump out and bust someone. Another colleague chimed in singing the theme song to the now-cancelled show, *Cops*. "Bad boys bad boys, what ya gonna do, what ya gonna do when they come for you?" This timely tune got a chuckle from the rest of the participants on the call—everyone except me. I sat there with my camera off and my mic muted, enraged. In disbelief, I watched the lack of sensitivity and joking tone that missed the moment of what was happening to Black people in this country. I figured either they didn't know about Jacob Blake, or their privilege prevented them from recognizing the tone-deafness of the seemingly appropriate allusion to police brutality. This, however, was not inconsistent with the rest of the world as I was watching it. I had seen no breaking news stories on CNN or MSNBC. The shooting wasn't a trending topic on Twitter. Not until the riots broke out in Kenosha, WI, where the shooting took place. It wasn't until businesses burned and looters roved the streets nearly three days later that the attention switched the headlines from COVID to civil unrest.

Interestingly, still no word from within my company's walls. I hadn't heard from the CEO or the executive staff. No commitments or proclamations were coming from every industry or sector that interfaced with Black consumers. The lines of communicating care, concern, and compassion were seemingly silent. How could this be after so many industry titans had only three months prior declared "Silence, no more!" Was it all just a performative gesture so as not to look out of step with the moment? Was it just good PR to showcase the collective moment of white wokeness? Or was the George Floyd killing so unique in its lack of scapegoatability that not to say something would shine a beaming light on the lack of humanity of those who witnessed it?

I dare say that Jacob Blake's shooting was not brutal enough to warrant the outrage. A police officer shooting a man seven times in the back leaves room for debate. If the officer felt compelled to fire so many times, he must have thought that he was in danger, right? The accusations from white communities went in full force across the social channels.

"Well, he did have an outstanding warrant, you know."

"He had a knife in the car, it turned out, so the cop was justified to shoot."

"If he had just stopped walking away and complied, he would have never been shot."

All of the usual off-ramps that firmly secured the cognitive dissonance required to watch a man be shot and feel nothing was used wherever convenient. If this had been a white person in the same scenario, we know the outcome would have differed. This isn't conjectured. This fact was proven two days after Blake was shot when a seventeen-year-old white male named Kyle Rittenhouse shot and killed two protestors and injured a third.

Rittenhouse came to Kenosha from Illinois to "protect" businesses being destroyed by protestors. He saw himself as a militia member who was doing fine, upstanding citizen work. Let's ignore the fact that at seventeen, he should not have had access to an AR-15 style weapon and only look at the fact that he was present on the streets amid civil unrest, armed and ready to shoot. This singular fact is what separates Black from White in the eyes of law enforcement.

Now, if we fast forward and you stop at the moments right after he killed two and wounded a third, we find Kyle running towards the police with his weapon strapped across his torso and his hands up. You also see a trail of protestors following behind him, yelling to the police that this man just shot three people. As Kyle nears three police vehicles, not a single officer exits their vehicle to intercept him. In fact, they pull away as if nothing was going on. To add further insult to serious injury, Kyle was neither detained nor arrested that night. Instead, he returned to his home in Antioch, IL, where he was arrested the next day. He was taken into custody without incident—no beatings in the cop car or under police supervision. He was treated with more respect and dignity after committing six crimes, including two counts of intentional homicide, than Jacob Blake was while walking back to his vehicle to check on his son. That is the source of our outrage as a Black community.

It wasn't until that Thursday that the Black employee network at my company pivoted on their initial plans for our monthly meeting to open the floor for us to share our pain. Thank God for that platform. Many of us were suffering in silence and had not had the space to address our fears and grief. There were over 100 people on the call, but only about six or seven of us spoke. It's typical for this to happen as most Black folks are still unclear on how safe it is to fully express their concerns in open forums, especially those that have whites present. It's usually the handful of people who are courageous enough to speak up without breaking down in tears or going on a rampage that captures the majority of folks' sentiments on the call. I was one of those who spoke up. I called out the deafening silence from our leadership on this recent shooting and how isolating it is to be the only Black person in a meeting and listening to colleagues who have no clue what I'm dealing with.

Oddly enough, I wasn't even supposed to be on that call because I had opted to take the day off to heal. Calling out Black was the only way I could create enough space to work through my trauma without being bombarded by the oblivious insensitivities of my white co-workers. This is something I've encouraged my direct reports and mentees to do when they are faced with these same feelings of outrage and despair. It's nearly impossible to find the mental headspace or the desire to care about deadlines, reports, or deliverables when you fear for your safety or your loved ones' safety. This reality is something I wish white co-workers and leaders could understand. I would love to see more resources deployed for Black employees when we see ourselves being snuffed out by law enforcement. To have unlimited access to mental health care paid for by the company or a bank of days we can use to recover from these traumatic experiences would be a game-changing way for companies to show their care and concern for the Black employees. But as long as we approach the Black experience in corporate with the one size fits all approach, our unique circumstances will continue to be overlooked or, in most cases, unseen ultimately.

Chapter Five

CHOOSE YOUR STEREOTYPE: ANGRY, AMBITIOUS, OR AGGRESSIVE

As I write this, it's been only a few months since the murder of George Floyd. The energy of concern and compassion that rose to an unprecedented height in the weeks just after have seemingly faded into the background of white America's lives. The energy that encouraged a wave of white awakening and accelerated education on systemic racism and White Fragility has transitioned into the more comfortable realm of business strategy.

CEOs and executives from all industries scrambled in the first weeks to put out commitment statements and made pledges to end their silence on systemic racism. They pledged millions to support social justice organizations, made promises of increasing the hiring of Black talent from HBCUs, and some even suggested they would promote existing Black talent in their companies. The outpouring of emails, texts, and phone calls from white colleagues to their Black counterparts was the order of the day as if a siren call to comfort rang through the white community. These actions gave

Black folks a glimmer of hope. I sat on townhall calls with execs and their broader teams as Black employees openly discussed their experiences dealing with racist police, neighbors, and co-workers. I heard the soul-crushing accounts of dehumanization and the blatant disregard of individual personhood. For the first time, I even heard white folks recall stories from their pasts when they "unwittingly" engaged in what is now clearly identifiable as racist behavior. I heard white guilt, saw white tears, and felt Black pain, all for the first time in my career in corporate America. I remember a 66-year-old Black woman who grew up in Florida, saying she had never experienced anything like this in all her years. Then one day, the energy disappeared.

Due to the work I'd been doing with our Black employee network for a year and a half, I was one of the more prominent voices in the fray. I had made a name for myself in the organization by developing a documentary-style film project for our IT division. The intent was to leverage the films to attract Black and Brown talent. We did a major release of the films by hosting a red carpet event and inviting the entire headquarters campus to watch at an outdoor theater we'd set up. We even had popcorn, red carpets with "paparazzi," and step and repeat backdrops. It made a significant impact, to say the least. This endeavor positioned me as the guy with bold ideas and a staunch advocate for Black and Brown voices within the company. Nothing like it had ever been done before, so the company didn't know how to take it. We filmed the premier, launched a major social media campaign to amplify and attract, and became the first posts in our company's history to be unapologetically Black & Brown.

Some were blown away and wanted to set meetings with me. Others were more reserved in their praises, as this was a threat to the status quo. I give you this background as the context for how I operate within corporate spaces. I'm an anomaly, a glitch in the matrix as it were. My role is non-traditional but sits within a traditional function. I'm viewed as a bit of a renegade to the establishment. I have consistently weaved culture into the work I do so we could have representation. I urged executives to consider several strategies to increase the representation of Black employees. I brought in diversity consultants, unconscious bias platforms and provided a critique of existing policies when invited. However, I didn't have the title of Diversity & Inclusion, so it never made sense to executives in the company.

Because I was appointed to the Black employee network's global leadership team and had been such a visible proponent of diversity and inclusion at the company, Black employees would often reach out to share what was going on in their departments. I heard countless stories of discrimination in hiring, dehumanizing engagements in meetings with white managers, and dismissive micro-aggressions hurled in colleagues' emails. A lot of these incidents were reported to staff relations, but rarely was there any recourse. The reality was that there was no recourse for any conflict that didn't present itself as overt discrimination by the letter of the law. This reality was one of the most challenging things to deal with because I would share these accounts with higher-ups, and they'd just point me back to policy and procedure. This maddening existence of witnessing slights and injustices while yelling at the top of your lungs in a room full of deaf executives drives Black employees crazy and out of your companies.

All of these things were at the forefront for me when George Floyd met his fateful end. The truths most of my white counterparts had only come to learn in the early weeks post-murder, I had known all my life. My Black colleagues had known all their lives. This display of white control over the Black body and life outcomes was nothing new to us. So, when you made open commitments, showed care and concern like never before, we took it seriously. We felt there was a small window of opportunity to swing for the fences of change. I was one of those voices which rose to the occasion and began blogging vigorously on LinkedIn. I would have seven to ten conversations a week with white folks who wanted to see how I was doing and showcase their compassion. These accounts would provide me the necessary intelligence I required to formulate allyship guidebooks in the form of articles. These articles began to circulate on external channels and internal company channels alike. I had people reaching out to me to speak at staff meetings and people from other companies inviting me to speak at their Black employee resource group meetings. Someone told me that in almost every meeting they had where race and social justice were the topics, my name and articles would come up. As a result of all my work to raise white allies' cultural competency, opportunities knocked. Below is one of the articles I wrote to consolidate the learning I'd collected as a result of all the conversations I had with my non-Black counterparts. I crafted it to reduce the number of conversations and to provide a reference guide on how to engage as an ally.

Allies: If You Really Want to Help, Start Here

Thank you to all of the folks in my network who have reached out to ask how I and my family are doing. Thank you for your honest concern and genuine desire to know how you can help. To be honest, it's tough for those who are the victims of trauma to be put in a position of helping someone else. It's exhausting. But I'm always one to look towards solutions and will provide you with some things I think could help you showcase your commitment to being part of the change.

1. Read *White Fragility* by Robin DiAngelo. This will enable you to understand your own socialization and the systemic behaviors that are counterproductive to equity and meaningful change. I don't care how many Black friends you have, where you were raised, or if you marched in the '60s. YOU and your executive leadership teams need to read this!!! Shouts out to Patty Dingle, Global Diversity & Inclusion Leader at Visa who has recommended that this becomes mandatory reading for their executive leadership team. There's a reason this is a best seller and also why it's currently out of stock on Amazon which is pretty hard to do since Amazon has everything.

2. Work with your CEO, HR, Legal, and Compliance leadership to make #UnconsciousBias training mandatory. The policies in your company are written to address overt racism and blatant racial discrimination. However, it's the micro-aggressions, dismissive and dehumanizing tone, exclusion, being called angry, aggressive, loud, imposing, or intimidating that we deal with on a daily basis that erodes psychological safety, perpetuates toxic culture, and increases stress and health issues for Black employees.

To take it a step further, racial discrimination is one of the hardest things to prove and even harder to win in a court case. Don't believe me? According to Berry, Nelson, and Neilsen in their book, *Rights On Trial:*

How Workplace Discrimination Law Perpetuates Inequality," only 15% of cases brought before the EEOC receive a favorable outcome. About 5,000 cases are eventually filed in federal court as discrimination charges. They estimate that only 0.13% of potential lawsuits ever occur. So, when your staff relations or HR investigators wonder why Black employees are hesitant to speak up when we experience discrimination, it's for this reason. We know there's little recourse other than to take the case to the EEOC and at best you'll lose your job and get a payout (Median of $30,000 in most cases) and be left to deal with the trauma of having to document, litigate, become unemployed, and then move on to the next company and hope it doesn't happen again. All while the company doesn't have to admit guilt and will make you sign a confidentiality agreement.

Be courageous and work to go beyond the minimal legal requirements. Include training and education. Then go one step further and define consequences and accountability measures for those who do not uphold the values that create inclusive cultures at your companies. If you're complicit in allowing these daily acts of subversive racism to occur then you can leave your ally card at the front desk.

3. Make a list of how you will use your privilege, connections, voice, and power to influence change at local community levels, within your companies, and

within your own households. Share this list with a Black colleague or friend that you have a trusting relationship with and see what they think. Be open to the feedback and welcome the dialogue. Once you've done this, share that list with a few of your trusted white friends, family members, or colleagues. Since you will have read *White Fragility*, you will be able to tell quite quickly where they are in their journey and be able to help advance their knowledge on the subject. With enough of these conversations, you will be clearer on where your opportunities lie to leverage your position of privilege to influence change.

I've thrown a lot at you. I know it seems like a lot of work and maybe you're not willing to do it. That's fine. But remember the things we as Black people in this country, in our neighborhoods, in our workplaces, go through on a daily basis and ask yourself if the above is nearly as hard. For the percentage of you who will commit to the solutions above, I applaud your courage, your bravery, and your allyship. These actions may cause rifts in relationships with people you've known for years or even family members. I can't promise you it will be easy, but I can promise you it will be worth it. Godspeed.

One morning I received a meeting request from the administrative assistant of one of our VPs. The invite came in at 9 AM, but the meeting was at 11 AM the same day. Typically, when a meeting gets thrown on your calendar by an exec for the same day, something is either really wrong or really right. We hopped on the call and she started by asking me how I was doing. This particular VP was the only person of color on her leadership team, so I felt a sense of comfort and was more relaxed. She opened up about how she was feeling about everything that was going on since Floyd's death. She even shared a story of how she grew up privileged back home because she could pass for white. This story brought her to tears. As the conversation moved forward, she suggested a few things she wanted to accomplish during this time.

She began first by apologizing. I was baffled. "What are you apologizing for?" I asked. "Because you've been telling us these things from the day you got here, and we ignored you. We were too busy, and we didn't take it seriously. We didn't set you up for success." I was blown away. Nothing like this had ever happened to me in my seventeen-year career in corporate America.

Receiving an apology and an admission that what I was saying the whole time was falling on deaf ears was like receiving a pardon from the President after serving time for a crime you didn't commit. Next, she let me know she would like to revive the documentary about code-switching that I'd pitched last year but had been shut down by several executive leaders. Some thought the concept was too much for most white staff to wrap their heads around and cause too much disruption. She then asked if I'd like to join the Diversity & Inclusion team, which she oversaw. All of this was coming out of left field for sure, but I was overwhelmed with vindication. I accepted the verbal invitation and asked that we follow up to discuss details and timing. She agreed, and that was that.

In the following weeks, I would continue to push for change. In the first days after George Floyd, the company's Chief HR Officer (CHRO), reached out to me on my cell to check in and see how I was doing. In this exchange, she gave me her personal cell number and encouraged me to call or text anytime. She assured me that we could be real with each other and that she was there if I needed anything. I had a relationship with her from my first few weeks at the company. I'll never forget our first one on one when she asked if I would be comfortable giving her my perspective as a Black man. She was keen to know my experiences and wanted me to provide feedback on how we could make it a better environment for Black folks. That was a game-changing exchange, and I viewed her as an ally from there on out.

One day, after an HR all-staff meeting, I decided to reach out to our CHRO. During the call, the head of Diversity & Inclusion, a Black woman, had presented her strategy on how they would take the company forward on the journey of a more inclusive organization. Rather than ask questions in the public forum, I felt it more appropriate to engage via a text. I started the text message by acknowledging all of the great work done to advance the D&I initiatives. Next, I asked what we were considering in terms of structural change to support all of the presented behavioral changes. This seemingly innocuous question proved to be the match that lit a forest fire.

She suggested that the structural change might be embedded in performance management processes, mandatory training, and a potential bonus incentive, which I viewed as behavioral measures. I responded by thanking her for her response, and then I brought up a recent article by Korn Ferry, titled "Asleep at The Wheel." This article had a stand-out analogy of how behavioral change without structural change was equivalent to trusting drivers on the road to do the right thing without having traffic signals or speed limits. She then asked me if I felt we were doing the structural change. Since I wasn't privy to what was being discussed beyond the time she asked me what policies I'd change if I could, I really couldn't say whether we were considering structural changes. I shared with her that the level of "Whitelash" that was starting to present itself, particularly in anonymous chats during a recent executive leader's townhall where an employee or group of employees shared a few racist comments, was becoming increasingly worrisome. It was clear that the company's middle management layer would not embrace the behavioral changes willingly. After all, why would they if there was no consequence if they didn't?

At this point, her response was becoming a bit more pointed. She suggested that based on the conversations she had with Korn Ferry's Head of Diversity practice, everything we were doing was on the right path or, in some cases, ahead of the curve. We analyzed the language in performance reviews (Which I led) to examine Black employee reviews' underlying bias versus their white, LatinX, and Asian counterparts. We were reviewing Black leader talent for the first time as its own group rather than as part of a broader organization and reviewing supplier contracts, bonus plans, etc. By all accounts, we were doing what sounded like, enough. I acknowledged that these were all great strides forward, and I agreed we are doing advanced behavioral work. I bid her a good evening and let her know I looked forward to catching up soon.

The next morning at 6:35 AM, I woke up to a text that looked to be a continuation of the previous night's exchange. She suggested that my last text message was "A pretty good dig" and felt I was labeling all of the work she mentioned, behavioral. She saw them as steps towards structural. I responded immediately, assuring her it was no dig at all, but I admitted I was holding back a bit. I then explained that when I say structural, I mean the mechanisms of consequence that hold people accountable. The measures that deter the toxic behaviors that have made corporate spaces a nightmare for Black folks for decades. I admitted I have challenges accepting incremental change in race matters and that I was working on that. My primary focus was to address the outcomes for Black employees who were waiting on the sidelines with bated breath. The ones who were skeptical of the proposed behavioral changes that wouldn't protect them from their microaggressive managers who were dehumanizing, dismissive, and holding them back from advancement. The same employees who didn't know what it felt like to have psychological safety in their daily lived experience. These were the matters at the very heart of my question about structural change. I then acknowledged the medium's limitations and how this would be a better discussion over a phone call. I knew it was impossible to convey the urgency and the criticality of this discussion when tone and inference were made on the other side of the screen. That's when she hit me with a gut punch that would prove too much to bear.

She offered that I may want to consider my role as a positive agitator for change and how I want to make my long-term personal investment in that change. She suggested there are two types of agitators in the world. Some agitate and push, become fed up, and leave because the company doesn't "get it "fast enough. Then some determine the place where it is worthy of making change, look for the signs of whether a change is possible and push, and cheer. Then she advised that we can always "cherry-pick" something within a company that could be better and she believed we would make progress if we establish a set of integrated actions that get to the systemic issues over time. She closed by telling me that others may see things differently, and she's always open to listening to other paths. Still, she questioned if I would do the same or continue asking the questions differently until someone agrees? I was floored.

I couldn't ignore the imbalance of the power dynamic. After all, I was in a text message back and forth with the Chief HR Officer of a multi-billion dollar company who could end my career if I went too far. But I was enraged. For this white woman from the midwest who has never had to experience being Black a day in her life to call me an agitator, in deference to the history of that word and Black folks, was wounding. To suggest that my incessant push for change is misplaced and that I should look for what's possible rather than what should be was insulting. I couldn't begin to explain how infuriating it was to have a white person tell me that my request for accountability was a bridge too far. Just weeks ago, we were being put on centerstage to tug at white audiences' heartstrings with our painful stories and being invited into the personal lives and stories of white guilt. How dare my passion be mistaken for agitation when every other Black person and I in corporate America has had to recall the anguish of 450 years over and over again as white people finally realized they lived charmed and privileged lives. The sheer Caucacity to suggest that I'm unwilling to consider other people's paths towards change when my people have had to accommodate white's comfort ever since we were integrated into their broader society. She hadn't considered that I am only four generations removed from slavery and only two generations removed from Jim Crow segregation. She never stopped to think I'm the living dream and the realized hopes of my once shackled ancestors. I am the first generation of Black workers who were embued with the expectation of fair treatment and guaranteed protection from discrimination under the law in the workplace. And here I am, being told my inquiry about structural change is a bridge too far—a seeming affront to the common decency of work decorum?

It took me two hours to finally put forth a reply. My wife begged me to apologize, born out of fear of seeing her husband terminated for offending an executive over a text message. I complied and responded by saying I had agitated one of my champions and hoped she knew how much I appreciated what she and the CEO were doing to bring about change. I begged for pardon if I had offended or seemed unappreciative of how heavy a lift this must be for her personally and professionally. With that, the conversation came to a close. She never replied. I hated myself for apologizing.

In the next few weeks after this exchange, I noticed things starting to change. The invite to join the D&I team had gone cold. I hadn't heard anything regarding the new opportunity beyond a check-in with the VP who extended it. Admittedly, the team was still coming together, and the business was slowly allocating resources to support the work. However, there was no discussion on how I would be contributing. Then, after another few weeks, I scheduled time with the VP to catch up and discuss the path forward. I also wanted to bring up the text exchange that I had with her boss and to provide visibility and, more importantly, clarity on my position. During our call, she advised me of how others were perceiving my brand. She suggested that "my energy could be off-putting because I wanted to run at 100 mph." This coded language is saying that you're making people uncomfortable by asking honest questions about structural change. Your transparency is offensive to those who aren't comfortable with the amount of change you're forcing upon them. Your aggressive approach will make people who were on the fence about this whole diversity thing retreat into their comfort zones of the status quo. She mentioned so much more in this call, but the message was loud and clear. I'm far too ambitious to want this rapid change in a company that acknowledged they had a problem only a year ago.

Companies are like aircraft carriers that turn very slowly. However, I've seen companies throw out their annual plans and turn their businesses around on a dime in the face of a global pandemic. They appointed people to task forces, promoted individuals to director roles of newly created jobs, and even allocated funding and resources to challenges they never saw coming. So the precedent has been set that when a company considers a problem that they deem a threat to their survival, they will remove all barriers and support rapid change with extreme urgency. The daily lived experiences of Black employees have not reached this level of criticality. When Black women seek promotions, have bold ideas, or are outspoken, they are labeled angry, ambitious, or aggressive. When white men exhibit any of these characteristics, executives identify them as go-getters, highly motivated, and strong leadership material. For Black folks to advance in corporate spaces, we must exhibit meekness and humility so as not to create fear of competition. By labeling us as "rough around the edges" or off-putting and a laundry list of undesirable traits that showcase a lack of fit in leadership, the status quo remains free of disruption.

Chapter Six

THE ACCOUNTABILITY CONUNDRUM

The 57-year-old Diversity, Equity & Inclusion (DEI) practice is now an $8B industry. What began with the Civil Rights Act of 1964 has now become a strategic buzzword that companies use virtuously to appease shareholders and quell public scrutiny. While there have been advancements in executing strategies to appear less racist, the underlying disease has yet to be treated. Diagnosing the disease and treating the symptoms has become the end game for most DEI consultants, rather than addressing the root cause. There are surveys, data science-driven analysis, natural language processing, and artificial intelligence technologies that are deployed with surgical precision to report out on where your company falls on the DEI maturity scale and which departments are most in need of reform. With all of the options a company has, it's a wonder a solution remains elusive. What I've come to realize over time is that the solution is straightforward yet nuanced. It's the one thing that hasn't been done yet to remove the barriers to achieving DEI. The answer lies in a dirty little word called accountability.

I found myself meeting with a few HR business partners and the head of DEI for a major company's operations division. I was brought in to listen and advise as they determined the next steps in deploying their DEI strategy across a 7,000 person organization. There was a discussion back and forth about which layer to begin with. Was it the senior leadership team or the levels below them and work their way back up? Would they designate ambassadors and deploy a train-the-trainer model? How would they measure success once all was said and done? All of these were excellent questions in the sense that they were typical inquiries within a corporate setting. Roles, responsibilities, and measurements are a textbook play for defining initiatives, but this was no ordinary business initiative. You see, this was the first time anything like this was being done. The senior leadership had a mandate sent down from the executive leadership to figure out DEI and figure it out fast. The CEO's commitments drove this energy at the top of the year during the annual leadership meeting. Now the execution time was at hand, and those tasked to do the work forgot to consider one thing.

The conversation's participants turned towards me to garner my perspective on what's at hand. After listening intently for the better part of twenty-five minutes, I had a couple of questions. The first question I asked was if all of the initiatives were fully-funded and supported by executive leadership, and you projected two years into the future, who would be the intended beneficiaries of your work? There was silence. Then after a few awkward moments, one of the HR partners said, "Well, everyone, right?" This was a seemingly innocuous answer, as any logical person would want the benefit to be applied to every employee. However, the fatal flaw in that answer is that everyone isn't marginalized within the organization. To develop strategies that benefit everyone is effectively developing strategies that help those that don't need it and further marginalize those at the bottom. This has been the approach and downfall since the first post-emancipation legislation in 1866. Wrap up what's intended to help Black folks in a veil of liberal inclusion for all, which ultimately dilutes the benefit for those with the more severe grievance.

So, I asked another question. Why are we beginning our strategy from the top and working our way down? Why aren't we working backward from those most marginalized? Sure we had conducted surveys and held courageous conversations that showcased Black folks' traumas like a trending Netflix series, but that didn't mean we were acting on their behalf. These business partners hadn't considered that the initiatives they were spearheading were derived from the will of the most privileged and being delegated out to the middle layer and below to do the heavy lifting in hopes that it would benefit every person whether they were marginalized or not. This is what I call "Trickle Down DEI." The problem with trickle-down DEI is it doesn't work.

Much like the economic theory that suggested cutting taxes for the wealthy would lead to increased employment rates, consumer spending, and government revenues in the long term, it turns out that the opposite is true. Cutting taxes for the middle and lower-income earners would drive the economy through the trickle-up phenomenon. This strategy has worked to elect conservatives to high-ranking political offices based on the elaborate deception that they actually cared about the labor class they were exploiting. What's clear is that the comfort of those in power is paramount, and the concerns of the marginalized will be addressed with a broad sword rather than a scalpel.

The trickle-down theory doesn't work in economics, nor does it work in matters of race relations, yet it's the go-to playbook that has been employed for fifty-seven years. So how is it that the tried and accepted DEI methodology begins with the CEO? They say that culture starts at the top, but in nearly all cases, the top people are the least marginalized and the most out of step with the company's actual culture. So what ends up happening is the CEO lights a fire under their direct report's ass, and they in turn rush to activity, or what I like to call running with scissors.

The first thing that happens is they identify a Black person to head up the DEI initiatives. This person is typically at a Director, Executive Director, or Chief Diversity Officer level and usually sits in Human Resources. If ever, the role rarely has any teeth and never carries a P&L, so the likelihood of achieving success is limited from the very beginning, but that's not clear to the DEI leader at the onset. Now that they have been tapped, she will quickly need to assemble a team to develop the strategy and assign roles and responsibilities. Once the team is assembled, the newly appointed DEI leader will need to achieve some quick wins. It could be initiating affinity groups, updating their commitment statements to the internal employee base, or make external statements to the public. Still, whatever action is taken, it needs to be highly visible. Most will focus on training and curriculum because there is still a belief that we can educate our way out of systemic racism. Enter the Unconscious Bias training. This training will be deployed as a mandatory activity for all employees, which, of course, will ignite an onslaught of what we affectionately call "Whitelash." This is the phenomenon of white employees becoming incensed at the requirement for them to evaluate their biases and blind spots where it pertains to race. They will feel as if they are being called racist, bigots, or prejudiced. This will have the opposite effect of what was intended, and these employees will become further entrenched in their beliefs rather than engaging in the self-reflective activities required to bring about empathy and allyship.

Now the DEI leader will be so bogged down in managing the internal disarray resulting from exposing people who are not ready to face themselves in the mirror that the other work of developing a strategic approach on a global scale will become a secondary endeavor. That's when they call on the DEI consultant firm to come in and help. Remember, DEI is an $8B industry, so the price tag of whatever the consultants conjure up will not be cheap by any stretch. They'll come in and assess, prescribe, and walk away from the scene several hundred thousand dollars richer while not having to stick around for the implementation. But while all of this is going on, there's still a critical stakeholder not being addressed. Remember the marginalized employee who suffers daily indignities from her microaggressive manager? Where does she factor in all of this busywork that is supposed to solve her issues of feeling excluded, undervalued, and dehumanized? When was she consulted? How is she to gauge if a change is happening? These are the questions that all marginalized employees ask daily, while the trickle-down assumption continues to evade its supposed beneficiaries.

I started this chapter by suggesting there is a straightforward yet nuanced solution. It's wrapped up in a word called accountability. When I ask DEI practitioners or HR professionals how they define accountability when it comes to DEI, they default to an answer that entails roles, responsibilities, and measurements. Scorecards, to measure the increase in hires of underrepresented demographics. Employee resource groups and ambassadors to reinforce the strategies from the center, surveys to gauge progress, and so on. But when I ask them, "who gets fired if your DEI initiatives fail?" The response I get is, "No one." This is fundamentally the root of why DEI has not been solved in over half a century. There's not a consequence for a mid-level manager who opts out of creating a diverse and inclusive team. There's no clear deterrent for a low-level supervisor who dismisses her subordinates by taking credit for their work and denying them advancement opportunities. There's no legal precedent for the hiring manager who selects a less qualified white candidate over the candidate with twice the education and experience but has the poor luck of having an ethnic name. These are the ugly truths that companies have yet to acknowledge.

Imagine if the CEO of a major Fortune 500 company declared a zero-tolerance policy on microaggressive behaviors that created toxic environments for marginalized employees. These behaviors would include consequence measures that ranged from infractions on their employee record, adverse impacts to bonus and compensation, and even termination for repeated offenses. Can you imagine the safety level that Black employees would feel if they knew the company was so resolute in its stance on protecting them that it was encoded in the culture? Imagine what that would do for the employer's brand and the increased ability to attract diverse talent. It would send a signal to diverse candidates and encourage diverse employees to become the most prominent bullhorn marketers for the culture that makes them feel valued. I told you it's a straightforward solution. But the nuance is where this fantasy gets pulled down out of the clouds.

The reality is that if this CEO enacted such a staunch declaration, they would be bound by its mandate as well. The executives would not be above reproach and would knowingly be opening themselves up to scrutiny. This goes against human nature. Most people don't willingly put themselves in harm's way. It defies the laws of self-preservation. Therefore, we are left with platitudes from the c-suite that bear little resemblance to full-throated decries for change. Instead, the legal department advises against these unnecessary risks when all the company is legally obligated to do is make a good faith effort towards diverse and inclusive workplaces. A strong Equal Employment Opportunity Commission (EEOC) statement, manager training, and employee resource groups are the extent to which a company complies with Title VII of the Civil Rights Act of 1964. The devil, however, is in the details.

The likelihood of a candidate proving they didn't get the job because they had an accent is slim to none. The probability of determining the junior associate whose manager left them off the happy hour invite email was because they were Asian is almost impossible. It's one thing to follow the letter of the law, but it's another to hide behind the loopholes and suggest you're operating fairly. So I ask again, who is accountable if DEI doesn't work? Whose job is on the line if the team isn't diverse and the culture is not inclusive? Who will bear the brunt of adverse consequences if the most marginalized people don't become those most likely to promote the company culture to external talent? To date, there are no hands raised.

Chapter Seven

THE BUFFER CLASS REVOLT

By now, you've read a litany of books on the subject of race and privilege including, *White Fragility*, *Stamped From The Beginning*, *So You Want to Talk About Race*, and others that became obligatory to every corporate book club in the summer of 2020. Sales of the top books on the subject shot up 6800% in the two months following the murder of George Floyd, which would lead one to assume that with all of this heightened enlightenment on the subject, we'd begin to see a noticeable difference. One would even think there'd be a rolling wave of newfound empathy and compassion from those most privileged. However, in the first week of 2021, when the world was looking to start anew and turn the page on what some had declared a dumpster fire of a year, the world got to witness the storming of the United States Capitol by right-wing domestic terrorists.

At the time of this writing, the details are still being pieced together about what was known before the insurrection, who was involved in the planning and execution, and which political heads will roll as a result.

However, on January 6, 2021, what we witnessed was nothing short of the Buffer Class operating to the fullest extent their privilege would allow. The reason I call them the buffer class is founded in the earliest days of the inception of the colonies. Borrowed mainly from the European need to classify the various socio-economic strata within their realm, categorizing people based on their proximity to power was a default in the new world. Starting first with the indigenous people of the Americas and then the enslaved labor class, those who were identifiable as "other" were subsequently classified to make clear distinctions between the owner class and the labor class. But the nuance of race was injected to further create a murky distinction between the have and have nots.

Eastern European and Irish immigrants made up many of the early indentured servant population during the colonial period. Those who were working off debts from their former homelands, working off prison sentences, working on contract to help develop the untamed land, or those who happened to scrounge up enough to secure passage to the new world to explore new opportunities made up the community of the have nots as well. However, at a certain point, the enslaved and indentured labor population began to slowly rise to the point that well-founded fears were growing from the wealthy class about being outnumbered. This left them open to revolts and rebellions that would cost them financially and even cost them their lives (See Bacon's Rebellion). You see, for the first several decades of the new colonies' existence, there was little discernible difference between the indentured and the enslaved. They worked together, ate, and drank together, and both were able to secure freedom after their debts were paid off in most cases. This little distinction led to a collective problem for those in power as freedmen's conditions became increasingly untenable. The lack of steady work and deplorable conditions created a strong resentment and, eventually, a strong resistance.

At this time, the colonial leaders enacted a system of racial classification that would elevate European immigrants and their descendants as "White" and all others classified as non-White and African. For Africans, this came with a destiny of servitude in perpetuity and even applied to those who lived free in the colonies for several generations. The newly elevated Europeans became what we now know today as the overseer class or the Manager class. They were entrusted with ensuring that labor continued without interruption and that the English upper-class investors' profitability showed consistent returns. These were the individuals who could not cultivate the lands based on historical knowledge of growing crops in tropical climates. They also were unable to withstand the diseases that ran prevalent in the new world. Therefore, they were better positioned to become the buffer between those with means and those destined to serve as a permanent labor class. This designation came with perks, such as employment, housing, tools, land, and animals. All of the necessary components required to be self-sustaining and potentially elevate oneself to a new status in a new land were granted to those who were not African. This preferential treatment would serve as the foundation for the entitlement and assumptive superiority for centuries to come.

Suppose we fast forward several hundred years into the future and stop at the year 2015. In that case, we can examine how the entitlements afforded to those positioned as the insular layer between wealth and slave labor found a hero in a longshot presidential candidate named Donald J. Trump. I won't go into the backstory of this political anti-hero anomaly, but I will say that his advisors were brilliant in their approach, which was to stoke the buffer class's fears. The majority of those who voted for Trump in the 2016 presidential election were white men and women between the ages of 30-49 and mostly non-college educated. This description is identical to the profile of those in the 1600s who were tapped to be the management class for those in power. What the Trump campaign tapped into on a psychological and emotional level was the fear of loss of entitlement and special designation. For years, the ideals of diversity, inclusion, immigration, and globalization pounded away at the White American ego's insecurities. The buffer class resisted the notion that we were all equal in the eyes of this democracy in conflicts too numerous to count throughout the timeline of the grand experiment that is America. The civil war was one of the most notable examples of the buffer class's fear of loss being manipulated to the point of one of the bloodiest engagements this land had ever seen. It wasn't the poor white man who had the most to lose in that skirmish as the majority of landowning and slaveholding families in the south were generationally wealthy American aristocrats. Yet, most of those who died fighting for the right to retain ownership of Africans as a permanent source of free labor was the poorest southerners who belonged to whiteness's higher class.

The strategy employed by the Trump campaign was to remind the buffer class that they were the intended beneficiaries of America's precious promises. They were mentioned in the constitution when the words "We the people" were penned. It was them who should be offended by Black athletes kneeling for the national anthem that immortalized their birthright in song and ritual. The liberal left sought to take your jobs away and give them to a wave of undeserving illegal immigrants from Mexico. It was the lazy Blacks who made your neighborhoods unsafe and threatened your lineage's purity and survival due to interracial relationships. These narratives converged in a cacophony of social media and mainstream media outlets on a constant loop. The tools of the wealthy class were deployed in full force to shape thinking and mobilize fear into action, which would successfully turn the insecurities of the largest population in America into a real-life army of entitled have-nots.

The next four years of the Trump Presidency would provide the buffer class a sense of freedom to wear their true colors because they no longer had to hide in the shadows of political correctness. This wealthy multi-millionaire from New York City convinced high school dropouts in Arkansas and other middle-America states that they had something in common. He fooled them into believing he was the common man, just like them. That his success was self-made and steeped in meritocracy just like theirs was. He lifted the burden of their failures and gently placed them on all the non-white inhabitants of America that were rightfully their own. He even got them to believe that in the upcoming 2020 election, if he didn't win, it was because the liberal left stole the election and defrauded blue-blooded Americans out of their guaranteed victory. He said explicitly that if he didn't win, it was because the election was rigged. Now imagine what can happen when these messages get amplified by every social outlet and algorithm you engage with daily for hours at a time. The outcome is the weaponization of white insecurity.

For Black folks, watching the events of January 6 unfold was not a surprise, nor was it a shock. We witnessed the entitlement of the buffer class being weaponized and turned on the establishment that entitled it. We watched as the blue lives that seemed to matter so much during the protests that marked the summer of 2020 came under attack trying to protect the Capitol. We gazed at hypocrisy in rare form as white cis-gendered men and women broke down doors and smashed in windows to run the halls and occupy the seats of power in the Senate chamber. We saw former military members who took an oath to protect the country from enemies both foreign and domestic enter the building with zip ties, confederate flags, and even pipe bombs to which we still don't know their intended targets. This is the very terror that Black communities like Greenwood in Tulsa, Oklahoma, and Rosewood, Florida, had witnessed before. This was the not-too-distant memory of the Jim Crow south that my parents and grandparents still recollect with horror. No, for Black people, this was not a poor reflection of America, but rather a shining example of what America has always been to those it deemed as other.

What's more poignant for us as Black folks are the reality that many who were there to storm the Capitol are the very people we interact with every day. They're the teachers in our schools, the managers at our jobs, the police and fire department employees who patrol and protect our communities. They're the librarians, food delivery, bartenders, rideshare drivers, and grocery store clerks who harbor these feelings of rage and betrayal. These are the healthcare workers who fail to give adequate care to Black patients due to racist ideals of Black's inability to feel pain the same way white patients do. These insurrectionists showcased who they are and have been for twenty-two generations on January 6.

In corporate spaces, Black folks had to endure another day at work questioning their value as they watched white people escorted in and out of the Capitol building as they broke through barricades, killed a police officer, and breached the highest-ranking political official's chambers. All the while, knowing full well that if it had been a predominantly Black crowd, the bloodshed and use of force would have been swift and heavy-handed. Those who didn't storm the Capitol but cheered from their homes also sat in video conference calls, utterly indifferent to the plight of their Black colleagues and direct reports. We discovered that our executives made campaign contributions to some of the cheerleaders and participants of the insurrection while also putting out internal statements condemning the insurrectionists' actions. The constant barrage of hypocrisy we face in this corporate climate is, at this point, beyond comprehension. Yet, it's what we must deal with if we accept the unfair struggle between freedom and security.

Interestingly enough, if the buffer class took a step back and evaluated their conditions versus their political loyalties, they'd see they had more in common with the non-whites than they do with the wealthy class. They would recognize they are manipulated into viewing the Black and immigrant class as the enemy when they are victims of corporate interests and geopolitical power players. Giving up one's comfort goes against the nature of human beings to self-preserve. The sobering truth is that the buffer class will have to come to grips with the reality that's been strategically hidden from them for hundreds of years—they are just another pawn on the chessboard of the wealthiest 0.1% in a game they were never meant to control or benefit.

Chapter Eight

THE TOUGHEST QUESTIONS ARE THE ANSWERS

I mentioned at the outset that this is not a solutions book. I don't believe anyone who sells solutions and doesn't include the harsh realities of what I've laid out are interested in advancing the aims of real equity and inclusion, but rather only advancing their bottom line from book sales and training courses. However, I believe there are questions that executives and DEI practitioners alike could benefit from answering to test how ready they are to tackle the real issues that stand as barriers to achieving success. These questions should serve as thought provokers and conversation starters. I believe you have to examine your cultural competency and those tasked with executing the work if you want to ensure those most marginalized are the beneficiaries of the work being done. Additionally, companies that speak to DEI in lip service only stand to do irreparable harm to their employer brand and their corporate reputation for years to come.

Executive Readiness Check

As a readiness check, your executive teams should ask themselves the following questions:

1. Are we committed to no longer perpetuating systemically racist behaviors?

2. Who are the most marginalized people in our company when it comes to representation, ability to be their authentic selves, and advancement opportunity?

3. What are the pain points felt by those marginalized at our company?

4. What is our understanding of their daily lived experiences, and what have we done to empathize?

5. What training should we attend before we set people off to work on solving DEI? Educate before you activate!

6. How will we ensure our strategy works backward from those most marginalized rather than those most privileged?

7. Are we ready to measure success by the qualitative improvement of the daily lived experiences of the marginalized?

8. Are we prepared to invoke a zero-tolerance policy on microaggressions and toxic behaviors?

9. Are we prepared to remove the employees contributing to a toxic work environment, no matter who they are?

10. What consequences are we ready to impose on those who do not abide by an inclusive culture's mandates?

Recruitment For Cultural Competency

In earlier chapters, I examined the issue of inviting Black and diverse talent into burning buildings. One of the things I didn't touch on but is just as relevant is not inviting more fire starters into burning buildings as well. If your organization is serious about attracting and retaining top Black talent, you have to be mindful of who you're hiring to lead them. Culture starts with leadership and thusly, toxic leadership is what drives attrition rates up. After all, employees don't leave companies, they leave bad managers.

It makes little to no sense to espouse commitments to DEI while hiring low to mid-level managers who have a deficit in cultural competency. If you want your culture to change, you have to first stop the bleeding by not bringing in more status quo thinkers who perpetuate toxic work environments. What's more, you need to ensure your recruiters are educated on the varying cultural norms of the talent they will be tasked with sourcing and recruiting. Are they grounded in the historical barriers to fair and equitable work for Black folks in this country? Do they know the difference between poor communication skills and Black vernacular patterns? As the tip of the spear, recruiters are making decisions on who is and is not a "culture fit" based on their own biases and the implied white norms of the company. If these frontline talent assessors aren't equipped with the knowledge of the cultures they're tasked with seeking out and attracting to your company, you'll struggle to see the return on any of your diversity initiatives and further cause damage to your employer brand.

Lastly, your hiring managers need to be upskilled in cultural competency as well. In addition to being held to a standard of metrics around increasing diverse, equitable, and inclusive team environments, hiring managers should be required to go through a curriculum that informs them of the nuances of Black and diverse cultures. This would help to reduce the misconceptions about our qualifications, intelligence, capabilities, and fit.

Below is a list of questions you can incorporate into your recruitment processes when considering how to approach representation and culture change within your organization. These questions are designed to challenge the candidates, especially those that lead people and teams, but even more importantly, they should challenge the recruiters and the hiring managers. Those who make decisions throughout the candidate journey should be able to answer these questions for themselves and for their company with clarity and conviction. The inherent risk of not being able to answer these questions is that candidates will see through the performative statements on your career sites and call bullshit when the empty rhetoric is repeated by culturally incompetent recruiters and tone-deaf hiring managers. With the pervasive reach of social media, Black talent will take to the Twitters, LinkedIns, Glassdoors and many other newly sprouting outlets to leave reviews and levee judgment upon your company for all to see. They will identify your company as a place that is harmful to Black talent and encourage anyone who will listen not to waste their time applying.

CREATING A DIVERSE WORK ENVIRONMENT

1. What do you see as the most challenging aspects of achieving a diverse work environment? Follow-up question: What initiatives have you taken to meet such challenges?

2. How do you challenge stereotypes and promote sensitivity and inclusion within your organization?

3. How do you encourage people to honor the uniqueness of each individual?

4. If you were hired, how would you use this position to increase or enhance diversity?

5. Please tell us about an instance when you have demonstrated leadership or commitment to equity in your work.

6. How have your experiences prepared you to advance our institution's commitment to diversity and inclusion?

7. Please comment on how you will contribute to our commitment to cultural diversity.

8. Is there an example of how you have demonstrated a commitment to diversity in a prior role/situation?

9. How will you contribute to the organization's effort to enhance diversity in a meaningful way?

10. What efforts have you made to help achieve a more diverse employee base? If you have not directly been involved in a similar endeavor, how would you help our company achieve this objective?

11. How would you help create and sustain an organizational environment that acknowledges and celebrates diversity and employs inclusive practices throughout its daily operations?

Developing Cultural Competency

1. Describe your experience or explain how you have been educated to understand the history of historically marginalized communities in the USA.

2. Give an example of how you walk in the shoes of people we serve and those with whom we work.

3. In what ways have you integrated cultural competency into your professional development?

4. What is your definition of diversity?

5. Talk about a time you successfully adapted to a culturally different environment.

6. What have you done to enhance your knowledge/skills related to diversity? How have you demonstrated what you learned?

7. Describe your understanding of diversity, equity, and inclusion, and why it is important to this position.

8. If we were to ask your colleagues or supervisor at your current position, what do you think they would say about your diversity background, experience and contributions?

9. What areas of diversity do you think you have to learn more about and how would you go about doing it?

10. Please comment on the benefits of racial, ethnic, and gender diversity.

Working With Others

1. Tell us about a time when you changed your style to work more effectively with a person from a different background.

2. Describe a time when you needed to work cooperatively with someone that did not share the same ideas as you.

3. What have you learned from working with diverse populations?

4. How does your own identity influence how you engage with other racial and ethnic groups?

5. When interacting with a person from a different culture than your own, how do you ensure communication is effective?

6. How would you advocate for diversity initiatives with individuals who don't see its value?

7. When dealing with a non-diverse environment

or individuals with little experience with diversity, how would you approach making diversity relevant or valued?

8. What kinds of experiences have you had in relating with people whose backgrounds are different than your own?

9. What opportunities have you had working and collaborating in diverse, multicultural, and inclusive settings?

10. Describe how you function and communicate effectively and respectfully within the context of varying beliefs, behaviors, and backgrounds.

Leading Diverse Teams

1. Describe your experience managing employees from underrepresented communities.

2. Please describe how you would create a work environment that is welcoming, inclusive, and increasingly diverse.

3. How has your previous work experience prepared you for [working with] [leading] a diverse [team, organization]?

4. What experiences have you had with recruiting,

hiring, training, and/or supervising a diverse workforce?

5. What role has diversity played in your leadership/management approach?

6. How do you adapt your leadership style to meet the different cultures and learning styles of your team?

7. In your experience, what are the key factors that contribute to the success of employees from diverse backgrounds?

Conflict Management

1. Tell us about a time you took responsibility/ accountability for an action that may have been offensive to the recipient.

2. Describe a situation in which you encountered a conflict with a person from a different cultural background than yours. How did you handle the situation? (Please be specific)

3. Talk about a time when a co-worker made an insensitive remark and how you responded.

4. Describe a situation in which you utilized your multicultural skills to solve a problem.

5. How would you respond to a conversation between colleagues that was clearly offensive to others?

6. What is the most challenging situation dealing with diversity that you have faced and how did you handle it?

7. Give examples of times when your values and beliefs impacted your relationships with your colleagues.

8. Can you recall a time when a person's cultural background affected your approach to a work situation?

EPILOGUE

Plantation Theory: The Black Professional's Struggle Between Freedom & Security was written to speak for those who've been without a voice their entire professional career. It intends to showcase the realities that countless Black professionals have faced despite our best efforts to prove our worthiness of opportunity. But more than an exposé on my experiences and those who look like me, I wanted this book to be a motivator for Black folks to remember their value.

I desperately want the future generations of Black excellence to recognize how much power they wield and evaluate closely the benefits and the detractors of choosing to work in Corporate America. I want my children to read this book one day and reflect on their decision to enter the corporate ranks as an employee or as a student seeking to soak up as much knowledge on applying sound business practices to their own ventures. It is my deepest desire to see more young Black college graduates reject the premise of plantation theory mindset that says they must choose to work as corporate sharecroppers for lower wages than their counterparts and chase the dangled carrot with little hope of ever capturing it. Instead, they would see that Black folks could apply their brilliance, excellence, ingenuity, expertise, and cultural IQ to their very own businesses that can vertically integrate into other Black companies to create competitive industries on a global scale. I want them to shun the notion that they need to work twice as hard for half the recognition and a third of the pay. I want them to be emboldened to say no to added responsibilities without added compensation and advancement opportunities. I want them to imagine not what it would feel like to be the CEO of a historically white-owned Fortune 500 company, but instead what it would feel like to be the CEO of a Black-owned Fortune 500 company.

This vision for the future will require us to confront the struggle between freedom and security. Freedom isn't easy, nor is it comfortable. This struggle requires us to examine the value proposition of a bi-weekly paycheck and healthcare benefits in exchange for the mental gymnastics, dehumanization, and microaggressive gauntlets that we're forced to endure. We still have a lot of healing to do. Our constant need to showcase our net worth in the clothes we wear, the cars we drive, the homes we live in, or our proximity to fame keeps us at the bottom of the socio-economic rung of society while simultaneously perpetuating a cycle of profitability for the very companies we work for based on our expertise in consumption. These voids of self-worth must be addressed lest we continue to run on the hamster wheel that is the Corporate American rat race. We have a long road to travel, but I hope this book serves as sustenance that converts into energy for those ready to take the exit ramp towards being fully valued for their authentic selves, for their inherent strengths, abilities, and brilliance.

This book is also meant to serve as a veil remover for those in positions of privilege and power as they embark on a journey of abolition rather than allyship. It's simply not enough to express the concerns for racial equity after reading several on-trend books, having several "courageous" conversations, and attending a few unconscious bias training courses.

Consumption of the text within these pages is a commitment to ending your participation in the behaviors perpetuating inequitable environments. May this help you find your voice as you declare to your families, neighbors, communities, and companies that you will no longer be the sideline participant in a marathon of inequity. The person who only serves a cup of Gatorade to those running a marathon for their lives, only to return to the proverbial sidelines when you get tired. I hope this leads to self-examination, heartfelt contemplation, and reflective conversations with your innermost selves. May you uncover your own solutions so future generations will benefit from your privilege due to your awakening.

I hope this read has forced you to examine your own journey in retrospect and identified the opportunities you've been afforded. I hope through the stories of Black professionals, you've been able to admit that meritocracy is not a notion that applies to us, but rather is the very ideal that hinders us from advancement. I encourage you to sit with yourselves in reflective meditation as you consider the ways you will cede some of your power, privilege, and status to create equitable companies that live up to the aims of the commitments they make to the world. May your marketing to Black and diverse talent match the reality of the daily lived experience they will soon call reality as employees. May you hold yourselves accountable by asking, "Who gets fired if the most marginalized aren't experiencing the intended benefits of our DEI initiatives?" This is the dream yet still unrealized and the foundation of the ever-elusive diverse, equitable, and inclusive workplace. We appreciate your engagement in working on our behalf in the rooms we are still not invited to join but will one day no longer require your patronage to occupy.

Godspeed.

ABOUT THE AUTHOR

It is said that one of the hardest questions to answer in life is "Who are you?" Through self-discovery, failure, and success, I know myself to be a creative communicator, a connector of cultures, and a leader by inspiration. I believe in the power of human connection and I take pride in being the bridge between aspirations and opportunities for others.

Professionally, my passion is helping global companies discover the essence of who they are at their core. Through award-winning employer brand and employee value proposition development, I've found fulfillment in discovering innovative ways to bring the humanity of employee stories to life. This work has helped to redefine internal cultures and connect critical external talent to their dream jobs. As a content marketer, my jam is unlocking the hidden potential of authenticity and ensuring the right message, finds the right audience, at the right time, on the right platform.

As a keynote speaker, coach, and executive consultant, I engage global audiences on topics ranging from Diversity, Inclusion, and Belonging, the future of work, the power of personal branding, and employer brand activation through culture marketing strategies. As a result, I've been able to help CEOs navigate diversity strategies, executives develop a more authentic voice on social media, students land their first dream job, and seasoned professionals rebrand themselves to attract their next career opportunity.

My wife Sana, two beautiful children, John III and Marian, and me currently call the Los Angeles burbs home.

CPSIA information can be obtained
at www.ICGtesting.com
Printed in the USA
BVHW071100310322
632995BV00005B/306

9 781953 307590